Many scholars assume that all genuine religions are basically similar and that it is possible to define the sphere of religion in terms of some fundamental characteristic such as the 'sacred' or the 'holy'. In his latest book, Max Charlesworth argues, instead, that we must take the diversity of religions as a primary fact. Any religion is an active response to a revelation of the divine, and human beings receive these revelations, interpret them and develop them in a variety of ways. This diversity is not, he emphasises, the result of human sin or ignorance, but is a primary datum of religions: the sphere of religion is ineluctably pluralistic. To illustrate his thesis, Charlesworth considers a number of examples of the 'invention' of religion, ranging from Australian Aboriginal religions, to the Rhineland mystical movement associated with Meister Eckhart in the early fourteenth century, to seventeenth-century sects like the Muggletonians, and to Roman Catholic attempts in the late nineteenth and early twentieth centuries to construct a theological account of doctrinal development and also to formulate a Christian ethic.

RELIGIOUS INVENTIONS: FOUR ESSAYS

RELIGIOUS INVENTIONS: FOUR ESSAYS

MAX CHARLESWORTH

Emeritus Professor, Deakin University, Australia

CAMBRIDGE
UNIVERSITY PRESS

PUBLISHED BY THE PRESS SYNDICATE OF THE UNIVERSITY OF CAMBRIDGE
The Pitt Building, Trumpington Street, Cambridge CB2 1RP, United Kingdom

CAMBRIDGE UNIVERSITY PRESS
The Edinburgh Building, Cambridge CB2 2RU, United Kingdom
40 West 20th Street, New York, NY 10011-4211, USA
10 Stamford Road, Oakleigh, Melbourne 3166, Australia

© Max Charlesworth 1997

First published 1997

Printed in The United Kingdom at the University Press, Cambridge

Typeset in Baskerville 11/12$\frac{1}{2}$

A catalogue record for this book is available from the British Library

Library of Congress cataloguing in publication data applied for

ISBN 0 521 59076 0 hardback
ISBN 0 521 59927 X paperback

VN

'Grace is . . . everywhere'.

George Bernanos, *Diary of a country priest*

Contents

Introduction   *page* 1

1 The diversity of revelations   23

2 The invention of Australian Aboriginal
   religions   51

3 Universal and local elements in religion   81

4 The making of a Christian ethics   105

Conclusion   139

Index   155

Introduction

The four essays that are at the centre of this book are exercises in the philosophy of religion, that is the philosophical discussion of certain crucial issues that arise about the important but diffuse dimension, or realm, or form of life that, for want of a better word, we call 'religion'. The term 'religion', at least in its present use, is itself a relatively new one and most scholars agree that it is not a happy one. None of the great founders thought that they were founding a 'religion'; instead, they spoke of a 'revelation' or disclosure of the divine, or of a 'Way' of belief and living, or of a 'Law', or of the 'spiritual life', or of a life of 'perfection'.[1] Jesus, of course, spoke of setting up a new 'kingdom', or the reign or sovereignty of God.[2] Again, and more importantly, 'religion' conveys the wholly misleading idea that all the multifarious beliefs and practices and (to use Aristotle's term) 'phenomena' that we now call 'religious', have something in common by reference to which we can define religion and clearly demarcate it from other areas of human life such as the realms of ethics, or art, or science.[3]

---

[1] If it were possible, I would like to revive the ancient pre-Socratic idea of 'the divine', understood as an order of being which irrupts into our ordinary world. See Walter Burkert, *Greek Religion*, Cambridge Mass., Harvard University Press, 1985, pp. 305–11. But, alas, the word 'divine' is now hopelessly compromised.

[2] See James D. G. Dunn, *Jesus' Call to Discipleship*, Cambridge University Press, 1992, p. 10. Dunn notes that the Aramaic 'kingdom of God' is best understood as the 'reign of God' or 'God himself in the exercise of his *sovereignty*'. In this context one might recall Alfred Loisy's ironic remark in *L'Evangile et l'Eglise*: 'Jesus announced the Kingdom, and it was the Church that arrived.' See Bernard Reardon, *Roman Catholic Modernism*, London, Black, 1970, p. 76.

[3] See Hans Küng, 'The Debate on the Word "Religion"', in H. Küng and J. Moltmann eds. *Christianity Among World Religions*, in *Concilium*, 183, 1986, xi–xv.

DEFINING 'RELIGION'

Nineteenth- and twentieth-century attempts to define the religious sphere, in much the same way as Kant tried to specify the conditions that make possible ethics and aesthetics and science, have proved to be illusory, confronted by the extraordinary variety and complexity of the realities and experiences we call religious. One thinks of Rudolf Otto's characterisation of 'the Holy' or the sphere of the 'numinous', itself defined in terms of an experience of a 'mystery' which evokes a sense of overwhelming awe and at the same time a sense of utter fascination and attraction (*mysterium tremendum et fascinans*). Or, again, one recalls Emile Durkheim's category of 'the sacred', or Paul Tillich's later characterisation of religion as that which evokes 'ultimate concern', or the various attempts to characterise religion in terms of 'the transcendent'.

It is fashionable now to invoke the name of Wittgenstein and to say that 'religion' is what he calls a 'family resemblance' concept. Wittgenstein uses the concept of a 'game' as an example to make the point that there is nothing common to all the activities we call 'games'. Instead, there is 'a complicated network of similarities overlapping and criss-crossing: sometimes overall similarities, sometimes similarities of detail'. Since 'the various similarities between the members of a family: build, features, colour of eyes, gait, temperament etc. etc. overlap and criss-cross in the same way', Wittgenstein calls 'game' a family resemblance concept.[4]

'Art' is also a family-resemblance concept since we cannot specify any well-defined set of characteristics that all the activities we call 'art' – poetry and drama and the novel, music, dance, painting, sculpture and architecture – have in common. So also, 'religion' is a family-resemblance concept *par excellence* in that the various ensembles of belief and practice we call 'religions' – Hinduism, Buddhism, Shintoism, Zoroastrianism, Orphism, Mithraism, Judaism, Christianity, Islam, Taoism, Confucianism and their respective sectarian offshoots, as well as the myriad forms of 'primal' religions like those of the Australian Aborigines or

---

[4] See L. Wittgenstein, *Philosophical Investigations*, Oxford, Blackwell, 1953, sections 66–7. William James had already made a similar point in 1902 in *The Varieties of Religious Experience*, Cambridge, Mass., Harvard University Press, 1985, Lecture 2.

Amerindian peoples – differ from each other as radically as the art of poetry differs from the art of dance.

In parenthesis, the philosophical ways of life of the western ancient world – Platonism, Aristotelianism, Epicureanism, Stoicism, Cynicism, Plotinian neo-Platonism – were systems based on rational reflection, but they were also presented as 'choices of life' and 'spiritual exercises', as Pierre Hadot has brilliantly shown. In this sense they were 'religions'. As Hadot says:

> all spiritual exercises are, fundamentally, a return to the self, in which the self is liberated from the state of alienation into which it has been plunged by worries, passions and desires. The 'self', liberated in this way, is no longer merely our egoistic, passionate individuality: it is our *moral* person, open to universality and objectivity, and participating in universal nature or thought. With the help of these exercises, we should be able to attain to wisdom, that is to a state of complete liberation from the passions, utter lucidity, knowledge of ourselves and of the world. In fact, for Plato, Aristotle, the Epicureans and the Stoics, such an ideal of human perfection serves to define divine perfection.[5]

The idea of family resemblance does not explain anything; it simply reminds us that not all concepts are univocal concepts (like 'kangaroo' or 'triangle' or 'petroleum') denoting that the objects to which they are applied have certain characteristics in common and so belong to a definable class. So 'art' and 'religion' cannot be defined in the same way as we can define what a 'kangaroo' or a 'triangle' or 'petroleum' is. The best we can do is to draw, with a great degree of arbitrariness, rough boundaries around the many and various activities we call 'art' or 'religion'. We are *locating* the concepts rather than *defining* them. Because of this there will always be difficulties in deciding whether or not a certain activity is really 'art' or 'religion': is, for example, Marcel Duchamp's presentation of a bicycle wheel a work of 'art,' or are John Cage's randomised sounds 'music', or is Confucianism, or even a secular ideology like Marxism, a 'religion'?

If, then, 'religion' refers to a vast and ill-defined collection of beliefs and activities and practices and exercises related in complex

---

[5] Pierre Hadot, *Philosophy as a Way of Life: Spiritual Exercises from Socrates to Foucault*, ed. Arnold I. Davidson, London, Blackwell, 1995, p. 103. This is an extended version of Hadot's *Exercices spirituels et philosophie antique*, Paris, Etudes Augustiniennes, 1987.

ways, and if the various ensembles or beliefs and activities we call 'religions' are often radically different from each other, and if there is a large grey area where we do not know whether or not we should describe a given ensemble of beliefs and practices as a 'religion', it follows that the philosophy of religion has itself to be seen as an ill-defined and diffuse form of enquiry. It cannot be the business of the philosophy of religion to discover the 'essence' of religion or to determine the universal characteristics that all religions share, nor to analyse the meaning of 'religious language' (as though it were a distinct species of language or discourse), nor to attempt to isolate the characteristics of 'religious experience' (as though there were a specific form of experience that we call 'religious'). Rather, the philosopher of religion must proceed in an *ad hoc* and piecemeal way, reflecting on issues that arise about the things we call 'religious', resisting the powerful temptation to look always for what is common to religious phenomena and remaining scrupulously sensitive to differences.

INVENTING RELIGION

The four main essays presented here were written on different occasions and for different purposes. My observations on religion and revelation are made from a very high level of abstraction, and I make no attempt to specify how they might be translated into concrete institutions or used to critically adjudicate between religions. I am convinced, however, that future developments, especially within Christianity, will need to be along the general lines I have adumbrated, although there will also no doubt be what I have called 'pathological' or 'demonic' developments.

My four areas of interest – religious diversity, Australian Aboriginal religions, the relationship between the universal claims any religion makes and the local knowledge and lived experience that plays a central part in the formation of 'tradition', the elaboration of a Christian ethics – are, of course, very different. However, I argue that they are all concerned with what might be called the invention of religion. The four chapters are, as it were, soundings in the diffuse set of phenomena we call 'religion', and the rationale of the book is to show how the idea of invention operates in an analogous way in the four examples.

To speak of the invention or construction of religion may seem to be a paradoxical description, since religions are, to speak very generally, revelations or disclosures to human beings of supra-mundane truths by a God or gods or by an 'enlightened' or prophetic agent. These revelations are seen as pure acts of grace. From this point of view, it might be said, there is very little room for human initiatives or interventions; our part is simply to receive passively the gratuitous revelation and to follow its commands. But to speak of the *invention* of religion conveys the impression that we play an active part in its production or fabrication, as we do, for example, in developing languages.

Of course, philosophical sceptics of various persuasions have argued that religions are 'man-made' fantasies and, in this sense, are totally invented. On metaphysical grounds, the story goes, there really cannot be any supra-natural realm of reality and experience, and religion is therefore an illusion. The world of empirical facts is the only reality there is, and scientific knowledge of those facts is the only valid form of human knowledge, and all claims that religion provides a supra-scientific mode of knowledge are mere obscurantism and superstition. We invent or make up or construct religions for our own purposes: to provide meaning and hope in a meaningless and indifferent universe ('a heart in a heartless world'), to cope with personal and social alienation and the prospect of death, to explain natural phenomena (such as chance events) that resist scientific explanation, and so on.

Thus, for Feuerbach and Marx and Nietzsche, we create 'God' in order to avoid or escape the existential situation in which we find ourselves as human beings – alone in a world which has no intrinsic meaning or purpose or value and realising that we are totally responsible for ourselves and for creating our own morality. If we are to assume that responsibility, we must (symbolically) bring about the 'death of God'. Or again, for Freud, religion (all religion!) has its origins in neurotic infantile fantasies by means of which we seek to regain a 'heavenly' father and escape responsibility for our own lives. As Sartre argues: all religion is a game of 'bad faith' or self-deception by which we attempt to evade the burden of being free and autonomous beings who have to determine, and be responsible for, our destinies. Not only is religion an invention, it is a malign invention by means of which human beings systematically deceive themselves.

This story is a familiar one and, of course, still a powerful 'myth' in our culture. But the kind of ideological secularism which is its source and which has held sway in western cultures since the eighteenth century, is showing signs of decay and exhaustion and has certainly lost a good deal of its force. Of course, scientism of various kinds (the philosophical theory that scientific knowledge is the sole valid form of knowledge) remains a potent influence. In particular, evolutionary biology has been pressed into service to produce a new scientistic 'world view' which excludes any religious dimension.[6]

THE PERSISTENCE OF RELIGION

However, the view of science and reason and the philosophical theories of empiricism and positivism on which the ideology of scientism has relied, have all been subjected to damaging criticism, and the naive view of human progress as a continuing saga of the reign of human reason removing obscurantism and bringing about enlightenment and human freedom and equality and justice, is now no longer plausible. Finally, the secularist confidence that religion would, like the state in Marx's theory of revolution, simply wither away, has been denied by the persistence, and even proliferation, of religious movements of all kinds. Some of the major forms of Christianity have lost large numbers of adherents and undergone crises of various kinds, but by and large the Christian churches and other religious bodies (for example, Islam) have shown remarkable powers of adaptation and transformation.

---

[6] For a brash example see Daniel C. Dennett, *Darwin's Dangerous Idea: Evolution and the Meanings of Life*, New York, Simon and Schuster, 1995. Dennett does not expain why, if science itself and its method of enquiry are also products (as presumably they must be) of the processes of evolutionary biology, they should be accorded any special or privileged epistemic status and value, or how, in any plausible sense, they can claim to be *true*. For pertinent remarks see Susan Haack, *Evidence and Inquiry*, Oxford, Blackwell, 1995, pp. 137–8:

Science has a distinguished epistemic standing, but not a privileged one. By our standards of empirical evidence it has been, on the whole, a pretty successful cognitive endeavour. But it is fallible, revisable, incomplete, imperfect, and in judging where it has succeeded and where failed, and at what times it is epistemically better and in what worse, we appeal to standards which are not internal to, nor simply set by, *science*.

No doubt, some of these developments in contemporary religions are extremely dubious and some patently evil. Again, some owe their success to their being linked to ideological nationalist and anti-colonial movements. Further, the astonishing growth of so-called religious fundamentalism in its protean forms, and the wilder expressions of 'New Age' sectarianism, are ambiguous signs of religious vitality. It has been estimated that some fifty million Americans subscribe to a fundamentalist Christian faith: they believe that they have been 'reborn', that we live in the 'last days' and that the end of human history is imminent, and that the Bible is a fund of inerrant truth relevant to all the social and economic and political issues of the day.[7] However, whatever judgments we make about the authenticity of these religious developments, the fact remains that, by and large, religions have shown themselves to be extraordinarily creative in transforming themselves in the face of radical social and cultural change. No one can now take seriously the once fashionable neo-Weberian sociological theories about the inevitable secularisation of economically advanced societies. In more general terms, when one reflects dispassionately on the matter, the scientistic and secularist claim that religion is really and finally an illusion, despite the fact that it has been seen in all cultures at all times as a fundamental dimension of human life – indeed, as the central value of any culture – is itself an extraordinary piece of philistinism. Casually rejecting a whole world of religious life like, for instance, the immensely rich and various 4,000-year-old Indian tradition – Hindu, Buddhist, Jain, Muslim – is rather like claiming that the whole aesthetic order or dimension of human life is meaningless or trivial and can be dismissed accordingly.[8]

---

[7] See Robert Jay Lifton and Charles B. Strozier, *New York Times Book Review*, 12 August 1990, p. 24.

[8] On the 'ubiquity and persistence' of the phenomenon of religion see the recent work by Walter Burkert, *Creation of the Sacred: Tracks of Biology in Early Religion*, Cambridge, Mass., Harvard University Press, 1996. Burkert argues that, although there are no 'religious genes' which determine us to be religious, there are 'biological preconditions' behind many religious activities and attitudes (p. 22). 'Religion keeps to the tracks of biology' and these preconditions 'produce phenomena in a consistent fashion' (p. 33). For example, 'the impetus of biological survival appears internalised in the codes of religion. Following this impetus, there is the postulate of immortality or eternal life, the most powerful idea of many religions' (p. 33).

THE RECEPTION OF REVELATION

The human reception of divine revelation is not just a passive reaction but an active and creative process, since our response to a revelation of the 'divine' (the 'act of faith' in Christian terms) is, or should be, the response of a free and autonomous person. God cannot coerce us to believe in and accept his revelation: that acceptance must be the free act of a free person. It is, in fact, a traditional doctrine in Christianity that religious faith in Christ and commitment to him cannot be the result of coercion, whether benign or violent. In the actual history of Christianity (and for that matter in other religions) that doctrine has been, no doubt, more honoured in the breach than in the observance. While giving lip-service to the autonomy of the act of religious faith, religious intolerance and coercion were justified on the ground that a particular revelation of God's truth *ipso facto* entails that other 'revelations' are erroneous and that one must be intolerant of them. After all, we have no obligation to tolerate religious error.

We now realise, after two millenniums of intolerance within Christianity (and other religions) how destructive that attitude has been. We are also aware of the paradox involved in any kind of religious coercion, namely that a person who is forced to believe is not really making a personal religious commitment. What does it profit a person if he or she is coerced, either directly or indirectly, to make a specific religious commitment? A forced commitment is no longer an autonomous personal act and has no meaning for the one who is forced, any more than a person who is forced to marry another really loves that other. Authentic love cannot be compelled by force (whether physical or psychological) and neither can authentic religious belief and commitment be compelled. It is, no doubt, because of the modern development of human values, such as the value of personal autonomy and the values of the liberal society, that we now belatedly realise this.[9]

---

[9] *See the Declaration on Religious Freedom (Dignitatis Humanae)* in Walter M. Abbott ed., *The Documents of Vatican II*, London, Geoffrey Chapman, 1966, pp. 672–700. In his recent work *The Gift of Death*, University of Chicago Press, 1995, Jacques Derrida, commenting on the work of the Czech thinker Jan Patocka, draws a strict distinction between the demonic, 'an experience of the sacred as an enthusiasm or fervor for fusion . . . a form of demonic rapture that has as its effect . . . the loss of the sense or consciousness of responsibility', and

If we reject the now discredited secularist views of the invention of religion, there is still an important sense in which religions are human constructions or inventions, since any revelation coming from a supra-natural source always has to be *received* and appropriated by human beings and is inevitably mediated by that fact. The medieval scholastic principle, 'whatever is received is received according to the mode or capacity of the recipient', directly applies here. In a completely obvious sense, which does not involve any kind of subjectivism, any revelation is what its recipients make of it. As already noted, the free assent of authentic religious faith is not just a quasi-passive assent to a body of teaching, but a creative appropriation and development of the revelation. This is a common sense point and it is not necessary to invoke any sophisticated theory of 'reception hermeneutics' to justify it.[10]

In parenthesis, it will be obvious that I am using the concept of revelation in the most general sense. Within contemporary Christian theology there has been a large debate about different 'models' of revelation – as a narrative of sacred history, as a body or system of sacred truths, as a vehicle of religious experience, as a means of transforming our human perspectives on reality and life and bringing about a 'new awareness'.[11] However, this book is not directly concerned with such specific theories about the nature of religious revelation: its theme is rather the dialectical interplay between religious revelations and the creative human appropriation of, and response to, and development of, those acts of grace.

A corollary of this point is that any revelation has to be *interpreted* in human terms. It has to be expressed in human languages and in terms of human philosophical categories and of particular cultural contexts. In other words, it has to be localised in order to become liveable. In a sense, God, or the gods, or any other supra-natural

authentic religious commitment based upon 'the responsibility of a free self'. 'In the authentic sense of the word, religion comes into being the moment that the experience of responsibility extracts itself from that form of secrecy called demonic mystery' ibid. pp. 2–3.

[10] See, for example, Hans Robert Jauss, *Question and Answer: Forms of Dialogic Understanding*, Minneapolis, University of Minnesota Press, 1989. See also Francis Schüssler Fiorenza, 'The Crisis of Scriptural Authority: Interpretation and Reception', *Interpretation*, 44, 1990, 353–68.

[11] See the excellent survey by Avery Dulles, *Models of Revelation*, New York, Orbis Books, 1992.

agency, cannot speak to us directly or immediately; their voices must always necessarily be mediated by human interpretation. Similarly, the voices of divinely appointed mediators – Moses, Jesus, Muhammad, the Buddha – have also themselves to be interpreted and mediated. Even if an angel were to speak to me and give me a message from some divine source, I must receive it and interpret it for myself. I must make it *mine*.

GRATUITOUSNESS OF AUTHENTIC RELIGION

Religion then is, so to speak, what comes about when a disclosure or revelation of the 'divine' – or whatever we may call it – is gratuitously made to human beings and human beings receive that revelation and actively respond to it in the same gratuitous spirit. As the dying words of George Bernanos' poor country priest have it: 'Grace is everywhere.' Various ploys are used in all religions to escape the implications of the gratuitous character of authentic religion: by attempting, for example, to emphasise the miraculous aspects of religion which overwhelm or coerce our reason and our will (before the burning bush Moses has no choice), or to make it seem that revelation is in some way necessary or 'natural' (as in certain aspects of Plotinus' Neoplatonism[12]), or to claim that revelation is made immediately and directly to us through the very words of sacred texts such as the Torah or the Gospels or the Qur'ān. However, as has been said, authentic religion is the gratuitous human response to a gratuitous revelation of the divine. A revelation always leaves a certain range of possibilities open to us and we must freely choose between them.

From this point of view then, one can speak of the whole receptive and interpretive dimension of religious revelation as being humanly constructed or invented, so that any religion is a product or resultant of the original revelation and what human beings make of it. As a contemporary Christian theologian has said: Jesus did not found Christianity: 'it was founded by Jesus' earliest followers on the foundation of his transformation of

---

[12] See Pierre Hadot, introduction to *Plotin: Traité 38*, Paris, Les Editions du Cerf, 1988, p. 27.

Judaism'.[13] Those early followers were in turn powerfully influenced by the interaction, at the end of classical antiquity,
between very different systems of thought and theological–philosophical 'discourses', Jewish, Greek, Roman, Christian. In this
interaction, new meanings appeared and new possibilities of
evolution of the original revelation were disclosed.[14]

The development of this interpretive–inventive perspective has
been very complex, and this is not the place to trace its history.[15]
However, among the various factors which played a part, one
might mention theological–philosophical theories about hermeneutics and the proper use of interpretation *vis-à-vis* sacred texts;
the modern critique of the Enlightenment and its conception of
universal reason; the allied attack on philosophical 'foundationalism' and the consequent focus on 'local knowledge' and traditions;
the influence of the various forms of sociological Kantianism
emphasising the role of social and cultural and linguistic factors in
our perception and understanding of the world (the 'social
construction of knowledge').

We should not, of course, take the idea of invention in a naive
and uncritical way. The metaphor of 'construction' has been
exploited so abusively in much modern thought (where almost
everything is, so it is claimed, 'constructed' – including the concept
of 'nature' and the 'natural' – the metaphor loses its power of
illumination) that we must be careful not to do the same with the
notion of 'invention'. There are many different modes of invention
– technological, theoretical, scientific, epistemological, linguistic,
aesthetic, ethical – but the two modes I focus on here and use as
models for religious invention, have to do, first, with our response
to an ethical situation where we have to decide what we shall do in
here and now circumstances (the creative process that Aristotle
calls *phronesis* or practical wisdom), and second with the very

---

[13] Stephen Sykes, *The Identity of Christianity*, Philadelphia, Westminster Press,1984, p. 20.
[14] See Pierre Hadot, 'Heidegger et Plotin', *Critique*, 145, 1959, 542:

> It is impossible to remain faithful to a tradition without taking up again the formulas of the creator of
> this tradition, but it is also impossible to use these formulas without giving them a meaning that the
> previous philosopher could not even have suspected . . . One then sincerely believes that this new
> meaning corresponds to the deep intuition of this philosopher. In fact, this new meaning corresponds
> to a kind of possibility of evolution of the original doctrine.

[15] For an overview of reception hermeneutics see Robert C. Holub, *Reception Theory*,
London, Methuen, 1984.

different kind of invention that is involved in the development and elaboration of a language.

It is often assumed that the development of the interpretive–inventive perspective has sceptical and subjectivist connotations. If we cannot know reality, including religious reality, directly but only in a mediated or interpreted way, how, to put it crudely, do we know which interpretation is the 'true' one? Obviously we end in a vicious regress if we attempt to set up some kind of final or privileged interpretation of rival interpretations, since we then need an interpreter to judge the final and decisive interpretation. But, if we have no final court of appeal outside the circle of rival interpretations, are we not left to the arbitrary views of the particular interpreter and so end in sectarian anarchy?

This objection is all the more serious in the religious sphere since, if it is true that we can only know the word of God (to use theistic terms for the moment) in a humanly mediated and interpreted way, it would appear that we are then submitting the infinite word of God to our own finite categories and language. Inevitably, it has been argued by Karl Barth and others, we fall not merely into subjectivism (and sectarianism) but also into a flagrantly hubristic attitude to God, where the finite creature stands in judgment on its infinite creator.

However, I do not believe that what I have called the interpretive–inventive perspective necessarily leads to philosophical subjectivism and relativism, nor that it leads to either hubris or sectarian anarchy in the religious sphere. To use an analogy: human languages are *par excellence* human inventions or constructions, but we are able to express objectively true propositions in them, and to communicate with other users of a language, and to translate from one language into another. Interpretation is needed at all stages of language use, and there is always the possibility of conflicting interpretations. But there is no final court of appeal (save in a pragmatic sense) in the event of such conflicts, which will hand down a final and privileged interpretation. Nevertheless, despite all the opportunities for mistakes and misunderstandings and misinterpretations, and the lack of any court of interpretive appeal, languages work successfully most of the time and we do not in fact end in subjectivism or relativism or linguistic anarchy.

THE DIVERSITY OF REVELATIONS

The theme of 'the invention of religion' opens up a vast terrain for reflection. Here, in this book, four aspects of this theme are discussed: first, the fact that there is a diversity of religious revelations raises many difficulties if we wish to maintain, as we must, that they all make some kind of truth claims. Some Neoplatonists see the fact that the One (the divine principle) is expressed in many 'theophanies' as a metaphysically necessary consequence of our human condition. We need to enquire whether the diversity of religious revelations can be seen in this light, or whether it is a philosophical and theological scandal that has its source in human ignorance and sinfulness, or whether (once we have taken account of the fact that religion is a human invention in the sense defined above) it is something to be expected so that the diversity of religions should occasion no more surprise than the diversity of languages.

In many ways, the idea that the diversity of religions is an unfortunate accident and that it will eventually be remedied so that some kind of religious unity will prevail, is akin to the ancient belief that the diversity of ordinary languages came about because some kind of original common language – a 'perfect language' – and linguistic unity broke up and produced the 'Babel' situation described in the Old Testament Book of Genesis (10, 11). Umberto Eco has recently charted the curious history of the search for the original and perfect and universal language ('the language that Adam spoke') from early Jewish and Christian thinkers to Raymond Lull in the fourteenth century, to Nicholas Cusa and Giordano Bruno and Leibniz and Kircher.[16] The search is, of course, a futile one, although interest in a lingua franca or an artificial language (like Esperanto), which would permit some kind of communication betweeen different linguistic groups, continues.

---

[16] Umberto Eco, *The Search for the Perfect Language*, Oxford, Blackwell, 1995.

It remains true, however, that we accept and live with the fact of linguistic diversity without too much trouble, whereas we tend to see religious diversity as a scandal.

The early Christians in the first two centuries gradually realised that the establishment of the Kingdom of God that Jesus spoke of was not going to take place in the foreseeable future and they were forced to adjust their theological perspectives in a quite radical way. We are faced now with an analogous situation by the realisation that the diversity of religious revelations is, so to speak, an endemic feature of religion. We can no longer believe that the present diversity will eventually give way to a situation of religious unity where one religion, whether it be Christianity or any other, is likely to become accepted as *the* religion of all humankind, or even that some kind of unified consensus will emerge among the major 'world religions' in the future. Mainstream Christian (and Hindu and Buddhist and Islamic) theology has not yet really come to terms with this fact which will require an adjustment and adaptation no less momentous than that made by the early Christian communities with regard to the advent of the kingdom.[17]

AUSTRALIAN ABORIGINAL RELIGIONS

Second, in the western world we have, notoriously, imposed our own cultural and religious categories and mind-sets on other cultures and their religions. Claude Lévi-Strauss remarks somewhere that the crucial difference between western culture and so-called primitive cultures is that 'we' have anthropologists and 'they' don't. Whatever may be the truth about that, anthropology is a peculiarly western invention and it has been used, wittingly and unwittingly, in the service of cultural and religious 'colonialisation', particularly in the case of so-called primitive cultures and their religions. The second essay is concerned with this issue with regard to anthropological understandings of Australian Aboriginal religions. Many aspects of the present received view (by European

---

[17] Though Hans Küng, in his recent work, *Christianity: its Essence and History*, SCM Press, London, 1995, has optimistically argued that the Euro-centric paradigm which has dominated Christianity until now is being displaced by a 'polycentric paradigm' which acknowledges the value of other religions.

scholars) of those religions are, it is argued, artefacts of a particular anthropological method and approach. It is also strongly argued that the religions of primal cultures, like those of the Australian Aborigines, can be just as sophisticated, and deserve to be taken just as seriously, as the so-called 'world religions'. The fact that they are religions of people living in relatively small and simple societies (hunter gatherer or agrarian) says nothing about their quality as religions any more than we can judge the significance of Christianity as a religion by the fact that it was founded in a remote and culturally unsophisticated outpost of the Roman Empire.

At the same time, we must not think that we can recover Aboriginal religions in their 'pure' state. After the white European invasion of Australia there was, inevitably, a new situation where the Aborigines' view of their own religious systems was profoundly and permanently affected. Before invasion there was a multiplicity of groups and peoples with their own cultural and religious identities; the consciousness that they were 'Aborigines', and that they shared a common Aboriginal identity, only came about through interaction with the white or non-Aboriginal majority culture.

This interaction, as far as the Australian Aborigines have been concerned, has not been merely passive in that they have been affected by the Europeans; it has also been active and creative in that the Aboriginal peoples have used the resources of the white culture, including the findings of European anthropology and archaeology, for their own cultural purposes. As it has been put: 'Aborigines will pick and choose those bits of archaeological histories that suit them, as they have already done with the evidence of 40 000 years of occupation. In this way they will continue to use archaeological interpretations of evidence to construct their own histories.'[18] That applies as much to Aboriginal religions as to other aspects of their cultures.

'Invention' then has a multiple sense here. First, Australian Aboriginal religions, like all other religions, are a creative and imaginative and 'developing' response to revelations of the divine made, in the case of Aboriginal religions, through the Ancestor

---

[18] Iain Davidson, 'Archaeologists and Aborigines', *The Australian Journal of Anthropology*, 2:2 1991, 256.

Spirits. But European perceptions of Aboriginal religions through the categories of late nineteenth- and early twentieth-century anthropology are also 'inventions' which have had a distorting effect on the way in which Europeans have seen, and continue to see, Australian Aboriginal religions. In turn, as I have remarked, the European perspectives have had a deep effect on the way in which non-European Aboriginal Australians themselves now construct their own religious histories.

UNIVERSAL AND LOCAL ASPECTS

The third essay considers the universal and local elements that are always in tension in any religious form of life. On the one hand, any religious revelation makes universal truth claims; on the other hand, a revelation has to be received and interpreted in a given cultural situation or context. In other words, it has to be localised so that human beings can *live* it. 'Tradition' is another word for this process of localisation. This essay examines the dialectical relationship between the universalising and localising tendencies in Christianity and the Roman Catholic Church in particular, and suggests that the same tension is present in Hinduism and even in Australian Aboriginal religions. If the universal element is too strongly emphasised, the vitality and creativity of a religion is compromised; on the other hand, if the local element is exaggerated, a religion can fall into sectarian anarchy.

In a recent essay, the Dutch Catholic theologian, Edward Schillebeeckx, has forcefully described this dialectical relationship between the universal and the local:

The gospel in its fundamental tendency and power is transcendent and universal and, in that sense, 'transcultural', by which I mean that it is not limited to *one* culture. On the other hand, precisely the universal and 'transcultural' gospel, which challenges all people and cultures, can only be found in the forms of particular cultures (the Jewish, Judaic–Hellenistic, Hellenistic, Carolingian, Celtic, Roman, African, Asian . . . cultures) – never above and outside them. There is no way of stripping off the skin and getting down to the essence of the gospel. Only in the concrete and in the particular can the gospel be the revelation of the universality of God and his salvation. In that sense, the expresssion of faith in the Bible and the Church's traditions depend on context and culture; they are localised and particular, while they nonetheless keep referring to the universal message of the gospel.[19]

Put in another way: we must be careful not to reify the categories of the universal and the local since the universal (and transcultural) elements in a religion are, in a sense, disclosed and developed only within the context of local knowledge and experience. (The gradual formation in Christianity of the scriptural canon as 'the word of God' through the lived experience of the early local Christian communities is an illuminating example here.) It is not a matter of first understanding (from a transcultural vantage-point) the universal message of a religion and then seeing how it may be worked out in the particular circumstances of a culture. As has just been said, we only know the meaning of a religious revelation *through* the forms of local knowledge we loosely call 'tradition'. I argue later that we are faced with a similar (apparent) paradox in ethics, and that Aristotle's ethical theory, where transcultural and universal ethical values are disclosed in particular and local cultural contexts, offers us a helpful analogy.[20]

A CHRISTIAN ETHICS?

The fourth essay is a critical discussion of the attempt in the Christian churches – especially the Roman Catholic Church – to elaborate a Christian ethics which claims to be on the same level as, and in competition with, the various ethical systems based on ordinary human enquiry. This is a well-traversed issue and it may seem that there is nothing new that can be said on it, but the focus of this essay is on how the idea of a Christian ethics has been used in the making of moral theology in the Christian churches.

Christianity, of course, proposes a way of living for those who believe in Jesus and accept his revelation. Jesus' Sermon on the Mount is the quintessential statement of what has been called his

[19] Edward Schillebeeckx, 'The Role of History in What is Called the New Paradigm', in Hans Küng and David Tracy eds., *Paradigm Change in Theology*, Edinburgh, T. & T. Clark, 1989, pp. 311–12.
[20] See Martha Nussbaum, 'Non-Relative Virtue: an Aristotelian Approach', in M. Nussbaum and Amartya Sen eds., *The Quality of Life*, Oxford, The Clarendon Press, 1993.

ethics of 'idealistic perfectionism'. But that ethic of 'heroic' or
supererogatory virtue presupposes an ethic based on non-religious
human enquiry and which is available – at least in principle – to all
human beings and not just to those who are committed to a
particular religious revelation. Confusion follows if the precepts of
Jesus' way of perfection are made into formal and universal
obligations or used to serve the purposes of the ethics of human
enquiry; even more confusion follows if the ethical imperatives
derived from human enquiry (as in the so-called 'natural law'
tradition of thought) are given the status of 'truths of salvation'. No
doubt, certain ethical modes of life, both personal and social, are
peculiarly consonant with the Christian way of perfection, but
there is no autonomous Christian ethics as such. When the
proponents of 'Christian ethics' actually engage in ethical discussion – about human sexuality and reproduction, justice, personal and social violence, death and dying, the poor and the rich,
attitudes to nature and so on – they are usually doing ethics in very
much the same way that everyone – Christian and non-Christian
alike – does ethics. The fact that they happen to be Christians does
not make their ethical reflections distinctively 'Christian'.

(Many Christian theologians have rejected this conclusion and
have attempted to show that, while we cannot derive a set of moral
rules from the Gospels or from the example of Jesus' life, or from an
analysis of Christian 'discipleship', it still makes sense to speak of a
distinctive Christian ethics based upon the 'character' or dispositions or 'identity' of Christians formed by their Christian belief and
practice.[21])

The conclusion, that there cannot be a distinctively Christian
ethics, has, of course, radical consequences for how we view the
discipline of moral theology within Christianity. First, it means
that Christians have to recognise and accept the autonomy of
what I have called the ethics of human enquiry and realise that
they have to rely on that ethics in the same way as others,

---

[21] See, for example, the work of the American theologian Stanley Hauerwas. *Character and the
Christian Life: A Study in Theological Ethics*, San Antonio, Texas, Trinity Press, 1985, p. 227.

Christians have their character formed according to the story of God's reconciliation with the world.
Consequently, Christian identity governs the moral judgments by Christians mediated not by moral
principles but by character.

Christians and non-Christians alike. Christians, and religious believers generally, have mostly recognised and accepted the autonomy of science and (apart from some exotic exceptions) no longer pretend that there is a Christian, biblically based, scientific view of the world. Again, most Christians have, more grudgingly, admitted the autonomy of philosophical enquiry and for the most part no longer speak of a distinctive 'Christian philosophy' (though they may hold that there is a Christian philosophical 'perspective'). In much the same way, I argue that Christians and religious believers generally must recognise and accept the autonomy of the ethics of human enquiry.

Second, my conclusion means that, in the past, moral theology has been encumbered with a great many issues it should not have been concerned with, and has been diverted from its true task of exploring the modalities of the spiritual life or the 'way of perfection'. The history of the making or invention of moral theology within the Christian Churches – especially the Roman Catholic Church – is an extraordinary one and the essay attempts to show how it might be un-made and then re-made in a very different way.

The four essays that make up this book are, then, variations on the theme of religious invention, whether this is displayed in the diversity of religious revelations, or in a quasi-pathological form in European attitudes to primal religions, or in the dialectical interplay between the universal and local (or traditional) elements in religions, or in the historical elaboration of a religious ethics in particular religious traditions.

CREATIVITY AND INVENTION

Imaginative creativity plays a central role in religious invention, the gratuitous response by human beings to the gratuitous invitation of the divine, and my four essays show how rich and unpredictable and subtle that response can be. Primal religions like those of the Australian Aboriginal peoples, formidably institutionalised religious traditions like that of the Roman Catholic Church in the nineteenth and twentieth centuries, the development of new forms of religious life among fourteenth-century

Rhineland groups of women religious associated with Meister
Eckhart – all show that creativity at work.

In a recent book on the Christianisation of the Roman world,
Peter Brown has shown that religious interpretation and development is always 'the art of the possible' where older traditional
elements are gradually reworked and modified and adapted to
radically new purposes, often in the most ingenious ways. Speaking
of the late antique pagans faced with the progress of Christianisation in the fourth and fifth centuries, Brown says that 'they were
impenitent bricoleurs. Hackers of the supernatural, they were quite
prepared to "cannibalise" Christian belief and practice, in order to
find spare parts with which to enrich their own religious systems.'[22]
That same process of religious 'cannibalism' was also used by the
fourth- and fifth-century Christians *vis-à-vis* the pagan world with
its belief in the universe, the *mundus*, as full of invisible spiritual
beings and forces, 'pulsing with the energies of life eternal'.[23]

Looking at the way religious movements are developed, one is
irresistibly reminded of the elaboration of new artistic movements
– for example, European Classicism and Romanticism and
Baroque, or Hindu or Buddhist or Jain or Muslim traditions of
sculpture and painting – which disclose astonishingly novel aesthetic possibilities. Indeed, the analogy between religious traditions
and artistic traditions is a very potent and illuminating one. Both
art and religion belong to the realm of the gratuitous and when we
make judgments about the value of artistic and religious traditions
we tend to use Jamesian pragmatic criteria where 'truth' is
measured in terms of the larger human consequences that the
movements or traditions disclose and open up. [24]

Again, it is impossible to demarcate a clearly defined region of
art. In certain cultures the category of 'art' includes not merely
paintings and drawings and sculptures, but body decoration and
tattoos and masks, 'the order of gardens, the spatial arrangement of
villages or dance grounds, or the moment of transmission of a

---

[22] Peter Brown, *Authority and the Sacred: Aspects of the Christianisation of the Roman World*,
Cambridge University Press, 1995, p. 67. See also Robert Markus, *The End of Ancient
Christianity*, Cambridge University Press, 1991.   [23] Ibid. p. 8.

[24] See William James, *The Will to Believe and Other Essays in Popular Philosophy*, London,
Longmans Green, 1903. See also the perceptive study by Robert J. O'Connell, *William
James and the Courage to Believe*, New York, Fordham University Press, 1984.

gift'.[25] 'Throughout the Pacific', an observer notes, 'the human body is a locus of artistic elaboration: so too are animals such as the pig, notably in northern Vanuatu'. Thus, on Ambae in Vanuatu, 'the most highly valued pigs are selectively bred hermaphrodites embodying a combination of male and female powers fundamental to cosmologies throughout the region . . . If art forms may be defined as modified or manipulated things that become aesthetic foci – in this region often, if not invariably, conveying sacredness and expressing political power – these pigs certainly count as works of art to no less a degree than the slit gongs and masks that are so widely shown in museum collections.'[26]

Further, if we survey the great artistic traditions, there is the same radical diversity between them as there is in the religious sphere. Even if we look at geographically and historically limited traditions such as Oceanic art there is the same imaginative profusion and aesthetic pluralism of movements and styles. And finally, as we have seen, the process of development within artistic traditions – a process of 'bricolage' pressing into service the old and traditional and the new – is analogous to what happens continually in the religious sphere.[27]

RELIGIOUS PATHOLOGY

Other sub-themes emerge in my four studies of religious invention including issues about what one might call religious pathology. When does a religious tradition 'go bad', or become hopelessly eccentric, or even humanly malign? What is the difference between what Derrida calls the 'demonic' and authentic religious commitment which 'presumes access to the responsibility of a free self'?[28] The various forms of denial, discussed in the essays, of the essentially gratuitous character of religion and of the role of human invention and responsiblity are of course fundamental here. Again, the refusal to accept the reality of religious diversity, with all that it

[25] Nicholas Thomas, *Oceanic Art*, London, Thames and Hudson, 1995, p. 19.
[26] Ibid. pp. 28–9.
[27] See the interesting remarks by Nicholas Thomas, *Oceanic Art*, p. 114, on the use of traditional tattoos – mixed with black-power and bikie motifs – by young urban Maori gangs in contemporary New Zealand.
[28] Jacques Derrida, *The Gift of Death*, University of Chicago Press, 1995, p. 2.

implies, is a basic cause of religious pathology, as is the exaggeration of either universal or local elements in religious traditions.
Finally, there is the effect of deficient philosophical theories and
ideas, as for example the philosophically and historically confused
ethical theory of 'natural law' in nineteenth and twentieth century
Roman Catholic moral theology.

I remarked before that the realm of religion is so diverse that the
method of the philosophy of religion is necessarily unsystematic or
ad hoc. Chesterton once remarked of Charles Dickens that he is
such a richly various and multifaceted writer that one cannot really
define his genius: the best that one can do is to walk around him cap
in hand. I suspect that, in the study of religion and religions, that is
also the best approach. We can only walk around the vast and
complex and ever-fascinating form of life we call 'religion' with
(critical) respect and wonderment. This is, in any event, the
approach of the four essays that make up this book.

The diversity of revelations

THE SCANDAL OF RELIGIOUS DIVERSITY

It is a brute fact that there are many diverse religious systems and that all of them, in one way or another, claim to be *true*, in some sense of that difficult word, as a body of teachings and as a way of life and as a 'revelation' or manifestation of the 'divine' or whatever term we use for the 'object' of religion. The problem is: how can all these religious systems and their 'revelations' be true since their truth claims very often appear to be incompatible with each other? Of course, if a religion made no truth claims at all but simply justified itself in a pragmatic way (i.e. whether or not it is true, it 'works' in that it provides a useful framework of meaning for life), the problem would not immediately arise. But the world religions – Judaism, Christianity, Islam, Hinduism, Buddhism, Taoism etc. – do make truth claims and do not *justify* themselves solely pragmatically, though pragmatic concerns do play a significant part in a believer's acceptance of a religious tradition in that the believer to some extent judges the value of a particular tradition in terms of the richness of spiritual life and experience that it opens up and the possibilities that it discloses.[1]

At all events, most religions claim that they are the custodians of a body of divinely revealed truths, and it is not difficult to see that there are conflicts and contradictions and incommensurable differences between the truths proclaimed by the various religions.

---

[1] Writing from a Roman Catholic perspective, Avery Dulles, *Models of Revelation*, New York, Orbis Books, 1992, pp. 16–17, outlines seven criteria for assessing the value of theories of revelation: faithfulness to the Bible and Christian tradition, internal coherence, plausibility, adequacy to experience, practical fruitfulness, theoretical fruitfulness, value for dialogue with other religions.

Most religions have ways of dealing with the prima facie scandal of religious diversity. At one extreme there is the way of absolutism and exclusion: *my* religious system is absolutely and exclusively true and is the sole true way of life, and this means that all other religious systems and ways of life are false in so far as they differ from my religion. In this view, the present regrettable situation of religious diversity and division has come about through sin and ignorance leading people to follow 'false gods', and when that is remedied diversity will vanish and true religious unity will prevail.

At the other extreme there is the way of relativism and syncretism (although these are not wholly apt terms) which sees the different religious systems as particular, and partial, manifestations or expressions of a set of basic truths. Reduced to their essentials the various religious systems all say very much the same things or, to use the familiar metaphor, they are different paths to the same destination. This is the position of what might be called 'vulgar Hinduism' and of the syncretism of Aldous Huxley's *philosophia perennis* and certain other philosophers of religion such as Fritjof Schuon. The title of Schuon's celebrated book *The Transcendental Unity of Religions*[2] epitomises this position: the inner meaning of all the world religions is the same even though they differ externally in the way they conceptualise and express that meaning. In other words, esoteric unity and exoteric diversity.

Between those two extremes (both of which, I believe, are unacceptable) there is a spectrum of other positions. To the sceptic, of course, the fact that there are many religious systems making apparently incompatible truth claims, and that there is no clear way of adjudicating between those claims, is a prima facie indication that all religious systems are false and that religion as such is an illusion. Just as the existence of evil in the world is a prima facie indication that an omnipotent and perfectly good God cannot exist, so also the existence of religious diversity is an indication that God has, so to speak, been remarkably unsuccessful in revealing himself unambiguously to us.

Awareness of religious diversity is, in a sense, as old as religion itself. The Old Testament is full of allusions to other religions – the

---

[2] *The Transcendental Unity of Religions*, Wheaton, Illinois, Quest Books, 1984.

Middle East was always the California of the ancient world – and Christianity was born into a world of competing religious systems. (It is worth remarking that the Old Testament acknowledges the holiness of many 'good pagans', for example, Enoch, Daniel, Noah, Job, Melchizedek, Lot, the Queen of Sheba.[3]) However, Justin and other early Christian 'Apologists' in the second century, while holding that Christianity was a 'philosophy', also maintained that it was not merely one philosophy among others but *the* philosophy. The truths that had been scattered and dispersed throughout Greek philosophy had been synthesised and systematised in Christian philosophy. Each Greek philosopher, they wrote, had possessed only a portion of the *logos* itself, incarnated in Jesus Christ.[4]

In the European Middle Ages the relationships between Judaism, Christianity and Islam were constantly discussed, and there is a genre of medieval theological writing under the rubric of 'Dialogue between a Christian, Jew and Muslim'. Again, European colonial expansion in the fifteenth and sixteenth centuries brought to Christians an awareness, ambivalent and distorted as it was, of the exotic religions of the Americas. Bartolome de las Casas, the great Spanish theologian of the mid sixteenth century, was one of the first to grapple with the theological problems raised by the non-Christian religions of the Aztecs and Mayans. (De las Casas argued against the Spanish settlers that they had no right to colonise the Americas solely because, as the settlers maintained, the indigenous inhabitants were not baptised Catholics.[5]) However, it was not until the late seventeenth and eighteenth centuries that the diversity of religions was taken seriously and seen as a *problem* for Christianity, and that sceptical arguments against religion based on the diversity of religious systems began to be developed.

---

[3] See Jean Daniélou, *Holy Pagans of the Old Testament*, Baltimore, Helicon, 1957.
[4] P. Hadot, *Philosophy as a Way of Life: Spiritual Exercises from Socrates to Foucault*, Arnold I. Davidson, London, Blackwell, p. 128.
[5] See Nigel Griffin ed., *Bartolome de las Casas: A Short Account of the Destruction of the Indies*, London, Penguin Books, 1992. See also Lewis Hanke, *All Mankind is One: A Study of the Disputation Between Bartolome de Las Casas and Juan Gines de Sepulveda in 1550 on the Intellectual and Religious Capacity of the American Indians*, De Kalb, Northern Illinois University Press, 1974.

On the other hand, serious theological discussion of the problem of 'religious pluralism' from within the religious sphere is a phenomenon only of this century. In the Roman Catholic Church it is, in fact, much more recent, with the work of the great Jesuit theologian, Karl Rahner, and the establishment of the Secretariat for Non-Christian Religions by the Second Vatican Council being the catalyst.[6] (One might mention that this recognition of the problems posed by religious diversity is linked to the earlier recognition of cultural and ethical pluralism. As Max Weber wrote in 1919: 'Forty years ago there existed a view that of the various points of view one was correct. Today, this is no longer the case: there is a patchwork of cultural values.'[7] It is worthwhile keeping in mind that the problem of religious diversity is paralleled by the problem of cultural and ethical diversity.)

I do not propose to engage here in a formal philosophical discussion about the problem of religious diversity. (There is now a large philosophical and theological literature about the problem – one thinks of the work of Karl Rahner, John Hick, Raimundo Pannikar, Paul Knitter, Henri Corbin and others – and an even larger corpus of 'pop' theological writing.[8]) Instead, I look at the question of religious diversity from *within* the religious sphere, so to speak. In other words, the question I pose is this: how can a Christian or a Buddhist or a Hindu, or for that matter a member of an Australian Aboriginal people, come to terms with the fact that there are other and different and incompatible religious systems in the world? What modifications in one's religious position as a Buddhist or a Christian or a Hindu has one to make in order to accommodate this fact so that a person might say, 'I am a Christian

---

[6] See the statement by the Vatican Secretariat for Non-Christians, 'The Attitude of the Church Towards the Followers of Other Religions: Reflections and Orientations on Dialogue, Mission', in *Bulletin Secretariatus pro non Christianis*, 56:19 (1984) 117–241.

[7] Max Weber, 'The Meaning of "Ethical Neutrality" in Sociology and Economics', in *The Methodology of the Social Sciences*, New York, Free Press, pp. 3–4.

[8] See Paul Knitter, *No Other Name? A Critical Survey of Christian Attitudes Towards the World Religions*, New York, Orbis, 1985; Gavin D'Costa, *Theology and Religious Pluralism: The Challenge of Other Religions*, Oxford, Blackwell, 1986; John Hick and Paul Knitter eds., *The Myth of Christian Uniqueness: Towards a Pluralistic Theology of Religion*, New York, Orbis, 1987; Peter C. Phan ed., *Christianity and the Wider Ecumenism*, New York, Orbis, 1991; Hans Küng and J. Moltmann eds., *Christianity Among the World Religions*, Concilium, 183, 1986; Willard G. Oxtoby, *The Meaning of Other Faiths*, Philadelphia, Westminister Press, 1983.

or a Hindu or a Muslim or a member of the Australian Pitjantjatjara people and I believe that the teachings of my religion are true,
but at the same time I recognise and accept the fact that there are
other religious systems and that other people believe that the
teachings of their religion are true?' In pursuing this question, my
method is what might be called reflective or ruminative, rather
than purely philosophical. I hope, all the same, that it might bring
some light to this whole issue, or at least remove some obscurity
from it by showing up false or illusory solutions to the problem.

THE ECUMENICAL MOVEMENT

One can get some preliminary enlightenment here by reflecting on
what has happened in the ecumenical movement among the
mainstream Christian churches since the 1950s. In this I am
following Raimundo Pannikar and others who have pointed to the
analogies between the attempts to cope with the diversity among
the Christian churches and recent attempts to cope with the wider
problem of diversity among the world religions. The ecumenical
movement has had a long and chequered history and, of course,
many fundamentalist Christian sects still reject its whole *raison
d'être*. However, a number of lessons have emerged from the
ecumenical discussions so far. First, the goal of unity among the
Christian churches is not strict or exclusive unity in the sense of
theological and ecclesiological and ritual uniformity. It is admitted
that there have been, and will continue to be, wide differences in
how the credal essentials of Christianity are interpreted and
practised in the various Christian traditions, though the definition
of what is essential and what differences are tolerable is a matter for
contention.

Second, there now seems to be general agreement that the
central theological and ecclesiological values of the various Christian traditions must, within certain limits, not just be tolerated but
be recognised in a positive way and respected as genuine, quasi-
autonomous 'developments' within Christianity. This kind of
recognition and respect has always been there as between the
western (or 'Latin') church and the Eastern churches with their
very different theological cultures, forms of spirituality and Church

structures, and it has now to some extent been extended to other Christian traditions. The implication of this is that no one Christian Church can claim to be the sole repository of Christian truth, although it may claim that it is a paradigmatic form of Christianity which, so to speak, sets the standard or bench-mark for 'orthodoxy'.

Third, an implication of the ecumenical discussions between the Christian churches is that genuine doctrinal and ecclesiological developments, in Newman's sense of that term, even of a radical kind, are possible in the future. The so-called 'deposit of faith' is not fixed and static (as the various forms of fundamentalism claim) but dynamic and open to change in the sense that virtualities and possibilities in the original 'revelation' are continually being disclosed. As Derrida and others have reminded us, the meaning of a text can never be circumscribed or defined exhaustively, and one can say the same of the meaning of the original Christian revelation. In a particular age or historical/cultural context, certain implicit possibilities or virtualities in the original revelation may be brought out or 'developed' in a way that would not have been possible in other ages or contexts. Take, for example, the contemporary emphasis upon the social justice dimension of the Gospel with its concomitants in the movement of 'liberation theology' and the idea that the church must be (in Hans Küng's description) 'the dwelling place of freedom'. Or again, one may consider the recognition of women's authority in the church as a similar development.

In parenthesis, it is because they are genuine developments, that is, making explicit what was implicit in the original revelation, though this is usually recognised in hindsight, that it is misguided to look for explicit intimations of the 'social Gospel', or liberation theology, or women's ecclesial authority in the literal text of the Gospels, or in the concrete details of the life of Jesus, or in the history of the early Christian church.

Fourth, ecumenical discussions have emphasised that the original Christian revelation is, as has already been noted, historically and culturally mediated. We know, for example, that the present systems of church organisation and government have all developed historically and in a culturally contingent way so that it is quite possible to envisage other, and radically different, forms or structures of organisation. Even those Christian churches which emphasise their continuity with 'the Church of the Apostles' recognise this. In addition, it is recognised that any particular historical/cultural form or structure of Christianity must obey the law of all such cultural structures, namely that certain benefits are always purchased at a certain cost. There are no 'perfect' structures where the benefits are unalloyed and unrestricted.

At the present time, then, the position of a Christian belonging to one of the mainline churches has changed quite radically from what it typically was fifty years ago. The Christian believer now has to say,

I am a Roman Catholic or an Anglican or member of the Greek Orthodox Church or of the Reformed churches because I believe that my church expresses the values of the Gospel in a paradigmatic or pure way. However, I acknowledge that other Christian churches (within certain limits) have developed the values of the Gospel in their own ways in their liturgy, spirituality, prayer, sacraments, theological reflection, church organisation and government, social concern etc., and I recognise and accept this. *In this sense* I acknowledge that I can no longer claim that my church is the sole 'true' church, although I still wish to claim some kind of special status for my church and its teaching.

To put it simplistically, in this view we will not know the full meaning of God's revelation through Jesus Christ until we have, so to speak, pieced together the jigsaw made up out of the various contributions from the churches and Christian traditions. (If one may so describe it, the 'true church' is a kind of future ideal limit or what Kant would call a 'regulatory idea'.) From this point of view, ecumenical dialogue between the Christian churches becomes not just an option but a necessity. To put this in another way, there has been a gradual recognition that the diversity between the Christian churches should not be seen as some kind of regrettable 'fall' from a primordial unity of belief – the result of human wilfulness and ignorance – but as a phenomenon having a positive meaning in itself.

I am sure that the various church officials engaged in ecumenical discussion would not subscribe to all the implications of Christian ecumenism I have been trying to tease out here. Again, for the moment I leave aside the question whether, philosophically speaking, the position I have been describing is a coherent one. I believe that it is coherent and that there are certain (limping) analogies with the view of science that has emerged from contemporary philosophy of science (for example, that there have been competing models or paradigms in science and that these models are relatively 'incommensurable').

However, I believe that we can use the insights gained through the ecumenical movement to confront the problems raised by the diversity of world religions. The problems are, of course, very different, since the diversity between the traditions *within* a religious system (within Christianity, for example) is different from the diversity *between* religious systems (between Christianity and Buddhism, for example). The latter is, of course, a much more radical form of diversity.

WHAT IS THE DEEP MEANING OF RELIGIOUS DIVERSITY?

As I remarked before, any religious believer has to acknowledge and come to terms with, and have some kind of theory about, the brute fact that there are many diverse religious systems with prima facie incompatible forms of religious belief and practice. What, for a religious believer, is the meaning of this diversity? Is it to be seen as just as an unfortunate accident, or something that has come about through sin and hubris and ignorance (compare the myth of the Tower of Babel[9]), or as an illusion, or does it have some deeper purpose to it? To put it naively, if there is a God what does God mean by it? What divine purpose, if any, does this variety and diversity serve? Is it something positively willed by God as part of a grand plan, or is it a consequence of what Christians call the Fall? What are we to think, if we are Christians, of the fact that Christianity appeared as an historical phenomenon some 50,000 years after (so far as we know) the beginnings of Australian Aboriginal religion, for example? How are we to explain the

[9] Genesis 11: 1–9. See the ingenious interpretation of the Tower of Babel myth by Jacques Derrida who sees God's 'deconstruction' of the Tower, meant to unify heaven and earth, as a deconstruction of the vain human hope for literal and universal unity of meaning: 'Des tours de Babel', in Joseph F. Graham ed., *Difference in Translation*, Ithaca, Cornell University Press, 1985, pp. 165–77.

religious interregnum between (to put it in a simple-minded way) the Creation and the manifestation of Jesus Christ? Again, if religion is a human phenomenon and comes into being, so to speak, with the appearance of human beings in the universe and has relevance only so long as human beings are about, can we speak of 'pre-religious' and 'post-religious' eras? I have been posing these questions from a Christian point of view, but of course these same questions can be posed, and have to be posed, in the terms of the other world religions.

The early Christians thought that the religion of the New Testament simply complemented and 'fulfilled' the religion of the Old Testament as though the latter came into being at the moment of creation. But, as we know, Judaism came into being at a particular historical moment, much later than Hinduism and Buddhism and Taoism, and much later still than some of the so-called 'primal' religions such as Australian Aboriginal religions. If, to use the language of western medieval theology, God desires or wills that all human beings should be 'saved', how was God's 'salvific will' manifested, and how were his purposes 'revealed', and what religious 'way' was available to humankind before Judaism and Christianity came on the scene? Even the most convinced and devout Jewish or Christian believer, who sees the Old Testament and/or the New Testament as 'God's own' revelation, has to ponder on what God was doing, so to speak, during the long historical gap or interregnum between the beginnings of humankind and the appearance of the 'chosen people', and later Jesus Christ's 'fulfilment' of the Old Testament. That period, when presumably 'primal religions' such as Australian Aboriginal religions flourished, must have had a positive meaning in God's plan; it cannot, for the believer at any rate, just have been a long period of divine silence and indifference. Any religious believer needs to have, one might say, some kind of theory about it.

Medieval thinkers pondered this question a great deal with regard to the ancient Greek and Roman worlds to which they gave an idealised status. For them, Socrates and Plato and Aristotle and Virgil represented a 'preparation' for the New Testament: they went as far as human resources would take them and they were 'naturally Christian souls' (Erasmus used to refer to 'Saint

Socrates') leading humankind towards the Christian dispensation
but, like Dante's Virgil in the *Purgatorio*, unable to take us fully, or
themselves enter, into the realm of grace. They saw through a glass
darkly what Christians are now able to see face to face. For
Michelangelo and his contemporaries, for example, the Roman
'sybils' were the prototypes of the Old Testament prophets, and
that is why those magnificent and potent creatures of Michelangelo's imagination play such a central part in the iconic strategy of
the Sistine Chapel.

No doubt, we can no longer think theologically in this way, but
we also have, in our own way, to confront the problem, or mystery,
raised by the fact that Christianity is but one religion among a
multiplicity of other 'primal' and 'world' religions. And, of course,
the same is true of the latter. Whatever their respective claims
about being the only true religion, they are not the *only* religion
and, as I said before, they need to have some kind of theological
theory about this.

One would have to say, however, that so far the problem of
religious diversity has been largely a Christian preoccupation.
Certainly, in some forms of Hinduism and Buddhism, quasi-
syncretistic solutions have been proposed (all religions fundamentally express the same truths) but that is in effect, as I shall argue in a
moment, to deny that there is genuine religious diversity and that
there is a problem about it. It has been suggested that the reason
why Christians have been so concerned about religious diversity is
(a) because of Christian guilt over past religious exclusivism and
'imperialism', (b) because of western liberal ideas about the value of
autonomy and (c) because of recent western ideas about the
'relativism' of culture and of human knowledge. As it has been put:
'Pluralism, with its view that every religion has its own particular
integrity, is a product of modern Western rationalisation. Pluralists
are modernists who think that autonomy is the highest good.'[10]
However, it could also be said, more positively, that Christian
theologians have been perhaps more self-critical about their own
belief systems and more open to the radical possibilities that
reflection on religious diversity discloses.

[10] Tom Driver, 'The Case for Pluralism', in John Hick and Paul Knitter eds., *The Myth of
Christian Uniqueness*, New York, Orbis Books, 1987.

FACING UP TO THE PROBLEM OF RELIGIOUS DIVERSITY

Put very schematically, there are a number of ways in which we can face up to this problem. First, as we noted before, one can maintain that Christianity, say, is exclusively the one true religion and that all the other religions are simply false: they are forms of superstition rather than authentic religions, or at best fumbling attempts to express truths which are expressed more clearly and fully within Christianity. Christ alone is 'the way, the truth and the life' and there cannot be other valid religious ways. Non-Christians must therefore be converted or offered the opportunity of becoming Christians and the eventual hope of Christians must be that all other religions will be absorbed in some way into Christianity. (As mentioned before, this position can be translated into their own terms by Hindus or Buddhists or Jews or Muslims.)

However, this is not really an adequate answer to the problem of religious diversity since, in effect, it denies the reality of that diversity, in that it makes it appear accidental and historically contingent, as though it could plausibly be held that the reason for religious diversity was simple ignorance and bad faith and that it could be remedied by more complete knowledge and good will. On theological grounds also there are conclusive reasons for rejecting this position, since it denies that God wills or desires that everyone should be 'saved' and that they have some available religious way of being saved. A kind of contradiction is involved in holding that God desires the salvation of all but in fact fails to provide accessible means for salvation. For example, if one held that only those who were baptised as Christians, or who had received the teachings of the Qur'ān, or who had the example of the Buddha before them, could be saved or enlightened, then all those who lived before the time of Christ or Muhammad or Buddha would be denied the opportunity of being saved or enlightened.

The second position of relativism and syncretism – all the world religions have the same essential meaning, though they express that meaning in different ways – is at the other extreme. It is, so I believe, vitiated by much the same objection already made against the absolutist/exclusivist position, namely that it does not take religious diversity seriously enough. Attempts to delineate the esoteric 'essence' which represents the 'real meaning' of the multiplicity of religious systems inevitably do reductionist violence to the various particular systems. Equally inevitably, the 'real essence' turns out to be so abstract and decontextualised and 'thin' as to be useless for practical religious purposes. Thus, for example, HH the Dalai Lama claims that the common essence of all religions is the idea that the welfare and benefit of all sentient beings should be recognised and promoted.[11]

The syncretist position also faces philosophical objections in that it simply assumes that the only way of removing the appearance of contradiction from the variously competing truth claims of the world religions is to suppose that they are really making essentially the same truth claims though expressed in different ways. However, this neglects the fact that we are not looking at particular decontextualised propositions in contradiction ('There is a God' / 'There is no God'; 'Jesus is the Son of God' / 'Jesus is simply a prophet or an enlightened one' etc.). The meaning of any religious proposition can only be determined by reference to a particular context or system, and it is not at all clear how one can compare, at least directly, religious systems and the 'truth' of one system as against another. (The situation is all the more complex in that those systems usually have philosophical theories of one kind or another bound up with them. One thinks, for example, of the pervasive influence of Neoplatonism within Christianity or of the Indian Madhyamaka philosophical ideas on certain forms of Mahayana Buddhism.)

As I noted before, one is reminded here of Thomas Kuhn's view about scientific systems and how difficult it is to compare apparently incompatible scientific propositions *across* systems and say that one is true and the other false. One is also reminded of contemporary 'post-modernist' criticisms of the decontextualised universalism which derived from the Enlightenment, both in the sphere of knowledge and the sphere of ethics, and of attempts to revive the idea of 'tradition' and of 'local knowledge'. What Alastair MacIntyre says of ethical or moral traditions can also be said of religious traditions:

[11] *The Bodhgaya Interviews*, ed. J. I. Carbezon, New York, Snow Lion, 1988. Though, of course, the Dalai Lama is not himself a syncretist.

A living tradition . . . is an historically extended, socially embodied argument, and an argument precisely in part about the goods which constitute that tradition . . . The individual's search for his or her good is generally and characteristically conducted within a context defined by those traditions of which the individual's life is a part.[12]

PARENTHESIS ON THE UNITY OF RELIGIOUS EXPERIENCE

The appeal to religious experience or 'mystical' experience, as distinct from religious teaching or doctrine or speculation, has always appeared attractive to whose who wish to find a common underlying essence in the diverse religions. Religious revelations may differ radically in their doctrinal expressions and interpretations and theological speculations, but the religious experiences that occur to believers and devotees within the various traditions show, it is claimed, a remarkable commonality or unity. Notwithstanding the immense differences in expression and interpretations between, for example the Buddha, Meister Eckhart, Rumi and Ramakrishna, they are all, it is said, basically reporting the same kind of 'experience'.

A typical version of this position is that of the English–American philosopher of religion W. T. Stace.[13] Stace argues that a perceptual experience, for example seeing a white object, may be interpreted in various ways: one person may interpret the white object as a ghost, another as a white sheet hung on a line, another as a white-painted rock. In other words, the self-same experience may be interpreted in three different ways. Stace goes on: 'If we are to understand anything at all about mysticism, it is essential that we should make a similar distinction between a mystical experience and the interpretations which may be put upon it by mystics themselves or by non-mystics. For instance, the same mystical experience may be interpreted by a Christian in terms of Christian beliefs and by a Buddhist in terms of Buddhistic beliefs.'[14]

When we look at the 'core' or 'fully developed' mystical experiences in the various religious traditions we find, according to Stace, that they all basically involve the apprehension of 'an

[12] *After Virtue: A Study in Moral Theory*, University of Notre Dame Press, 1981, p. 222.
[13] W. T. Stace, *The Teachings of the Mystics*, New York, New American Library, 1960.
[14] Ibid. pp. 9–10.

ultimate non-sensuous unity in all things'.[15] Stace cites the great thirteenth- and fourteenth-century Catholic mystic Meister Eckhart: 'Here (in this experience) all blades of grass, wood and stone, all things are One . . . When is a man in mere understanding? When he sees one thing separated from another. And when is he above mere understanding? When he sees all in all, then a man stands above mere understanding.'[16] This consciousness of the unity of all things is, Stace says, to be found in the religious experiences of Buddhists, Hindus, Sufis and Christians. In the theistic religions of the West – in Judaism, Christianity and Islam – the experience of undifferentiated unity is interpreted as 'unity with God'. But this is 'an interpretation and not the experience itself'.[17]

Stace's special pleading here is obvious enough. Any mystical experiences which do not fit his assumption that 'core' experiences are of 'an ultimate unity in all things' are explained away by saying that reports of the experiences have confused the basic experiences with theistic 'interpretations' of them. How, it might be asked, does Stace know that St Teresa of Avila and St John of the Cross did not, as they claimed, have experiences of God in which they themselves were clearly differentiated from God, but rather had an experience of the oneness of all things which they then misinterpreted in theistic terms?

Again, when Stace speaks of the 'core mystical experiences' he implies that we discover them by looking inductively at the various mystical traditions and noting their core characteristics and seeing that they are essentially the same. But, in fact, when we look at the various forms of mystical experience, we have to look at them in their total context in order to see what they mean. We cannot abstract the Buddha's religious experience of 'the void' from the total theological and cultural context which gave that experience a meaning for him and for others. And we cannot abstract Eckhart's mystical experience of being 'annihilated' in God from the total context which gave his experience a meaning both for himself and for others.

In actual fact, when we look at the different modes of mystical

---

[15] Ibid. p. 13.   [16] Ibid. p. 14.   [17] Ibid. p. 21.

experience in their respective contexts we do not discern an underlying common essence in them. Rather, it is the *diversity* of mystical experiences that impresses us. Stace's own a priori philosophical preconception that there *must* be something in common between the various forms of mystical experience causes him to neglect anything that does not fit that assumption and to gloss over the irreducible differences that exist between, say, Christian and Buddhist mysticism.

It is worthwhile emphasising this point with regard to Meister Eckhart who has been the darling of those, like Stace, who wish to argue that there is a unity of religious experience among the great mystics. At first sight, Eckhart's account of his religious experience – with its focus on the divine ineffability or 'nothingness' and the 'annihilation' of the individual soul in union with God, on 'emptiness' and the 'void' and so on – can appear to be Buddhistic and non-western. But, in fact, Eckhart's account of his mystical experience is an expression – albeit a highly original one – of a number of fundamental themes in Christian theology and philo- sophical theology from scriptural sources relating to the 'inhabit- ation' of the persons of the Trinity in the soul, the Plotinian Neoplatonism of the Pseudo-Dionysius with its 'negative theology', medieval Aristotelianism influenced by the great Islamic inter- preter Ibn Sina (Avicenna), and even theories about the influence of the stars on human beings. One of the best commentators on Eckhart, Alain de Libera, has, in fact, summed up Eckhart's teaching as 'a serene culmination of medieval Aristotelianism'.[18]

The fundamental philosophical objection to Stace's attempt to show the unity of religious experience is, however, that it makes the same assumption – that we can distinguish between 'experi- ence' and the 'interpretation' of experience – as that made by naive empiricism. Empiricist views of science, for example, as- sume that we can experience and observe phenomena through our senses quite independently of any non-observational or 'theoretical' factors. These 'theory-independent' experiences and

---

[18] 'Un couronnement serein de l'aristotélisme médiévale'. Alain de Libera, *Penser au moyen âge*, Paris, Editions du Seuil, 1991, p. 25. On Eckhart see especially chapter 8. See also the illuminating study by Oliver Davies, *Meister Eckhart: Mystical Theologian*, London, SPCK, 1991, especially chapter 9, 'Meister Eckhart and Christian Orthodoxy'.

observations are the foundation of all our knowledge, and we then build up our scientific theories and interpretations on the basis they provide.

But our basic experiences of the world are not, in fact, 'theory independent', since we can experience the world only within a context of non-observational or theoretical factors. These are not simply psychological and cultural factors – the distorting biasses and expectations of the perceiver or observer – but, more importantly, epistemological factors that derive from the nature of perception and knowledge itself. Our perceptual experiences have to be meaningful both to the perceiver and to other people, since we do not experience things in a vacuum and in decontextualised isolation and as 'brute facts'. And our experiences have to be expressed in a language which pre-exists, so to speak, our perceptual experiences and which enables us to make sense of our experiences.[19]

It is easy enough to see how this applies to the distinction between 'religious experience' and the 'interpretation' of that experience. Stace assumes that religious experience is theory- or interpretation-independent and that religious experiences are analogous to the basic perceptual experiences of the empiricist. We can, as it were, abstract religious experiences from their respective interpretive contexts – Jewish and Christian and Islamic theism, Buddhist atheism, Hindu pantheism – and then see that they are all experiences of the unity of all beings. But, as we have seen, it is impossible to do this. Religious experiences do not occur – and cannot occur – in a vacuum or in a decontextualised state.

BEYOND ABSOLUTISM AND EXCLUSIVISM

To return to the main positions with regard to Christianity's relationship with other world religions. The third position argues that, while Christianity is the paradigmatic religious and spiritual 'way', other spiritual ways also have their own value and cannot simply be rejected as false or as forms of superstition and idolatry.

---

[19] On observation and theory in science and the contemporary critique of the naive empiricist theory which closely parallels Stace's position, see Alan Chalmers, *Science and Its Fabrication*, Milton Keynes, Open University Press, 1990, ch. 4.

By following the way provided by their own traditions, or the basic moral law available to everyone, people can be saved as 'implicit Christians' or 'Christians by desire' or 'anonymous Christians', though what is valuable in those traditions can be found in a much fuller and richer and explicit way in Christianity. Christianity is the religious and spiritual way *par excellence* and the value of other religious ways can only be seen by reference to Christianity. (The great scholar of comparative religion, R. C. Zaehner, has, for example, argued that the theocentric tendencies of the *Bhagavad Gita* can only be fully appreciated by reference to the view of God that emerges in the central tradition of Christian mysticism.[20])

A similar position seems to have been adopted in classical Judaism. Thus Bernard Lewis, an eminent Near Eastern Studies scholar, says that:

> while Jews claim that the truths of their faith are universal, they do not claim that they are exclusive. Judaism is for Jews and those who care to join them. But, according to a well-known Talmudic dictum, the righteous of all peoples and faiths have their place in paradise. The rabbis relate that before the ten commandments given to Moses there were seven commandments revealed in the time of Noah, and these were for all humanity. Only two of them, the bans on idolatry and blasphemy, are theological: all the rest, including the prohibition of murder, robbery, cruelty etc., are no more than the basic rules of human social co-existence. Since Judaism makes no claim to exclusive truth, salvation, according to Jewish teaching, is attainable for non-Jews, provided that they practice monotheism and morality.[21]

(One might, perhaps, argue with Lewis' distinction between a *universally* true religion, such as Jews claim Judaism to be, and an *exclusively* true religion, since, if Judaism is universally true (true for everyone without exception and not just true for Jews), it must surely be exclusively true (that is, it excludes the possibility of other different religious systems being true).) Nevertheless it is clear that the classical rabbinic authorities saw Judaism as the central form of religion by reference to which the value of other forms of religious teaching and practice could be judged.

Lewis also remarks that 'from a Muslim point of view, neither

---

[20] R. C. Zaehner, *The Bhagavad Gita*, Oxford, Clarendon Press, 1968.
[21] Bernard Lewis, *'Islam and the West*, Oxford University Press, 1993, p. 75.

Judaism nor Christianity is a false religion. Both were in origin based on authentic revelations, but both are superseded by the final and perfect revelation vouchsafed to Muhammad in the *Koran*.' Lewis goes on to say that 'the principle has always been adopted in Muslim law and usually in practice that Christians and Jews – but not atheists, polytheists or idolators – are entitled to the protection of the Muslim state'.[22] Indeed, a contemporary Muslim scholar has said that

> there are those . . . within the Islamic world who realise that the destinies of Islam and Christianity are intertwined, that God has willed both religions to exist and to be ways of salvation for millions of human beings . . . and that Christianity is a dispensation willed by heaven not only as a historical background to Islam but as a revelation destined to guide a sector of humanity until the second coming of its founder.[23]

However, the main Muslim position seems to be that Islam is the central religious revelation, even though certain other forms of monotheism may have some degree of religious value of their own. (It would be interesting to know the attitude of Islamic theologians and believers to 'atheistic' religions such as Buddhism and 'poly-theistic' religions such as Hinduism and dualistic religions such as the various forms of Manicheeism.)

The third position represents a considerable progress over the absolutism and exclusivism of the first position, but it still stops short of according a positive religious value to the other religions and of recognising that God has revealed aspects of 'the divine' in other religious systems, and that authentic religious values which have not been developed within Christianity or Islam, for example, have been developed in those systems. As it has been said, 'what we are left with is a set of competing absolutisms, each of which claims to be privileged and, in some sense, to be judging the others'.[24]

'TOTUS DEUS' BUT NOT 'TOTUS DEI'

The fourth view attempts to acknowledge that other religious systems can have a positive value of their own and that the fact of

---

[22] Ibid. p. 76
[23] Seyedd Hossein Nasr, 'The Islamic View of Christianity', in Hans Küng and J. Moltmann eds. *Christianity Among The World Religions, Concilium*, 183, 1986, p. 11.
[24] Michael Barnes, *Christian Identity and Religious Pluralism*, London, SPCK, 1989.

religious diversity has a positive meaning. Thus, a Christian will hold that the Christian tradition has a privileged or paradigmatic status in that it is claimed that it is in the person of Jesus Christ that God has revealed himself most fully (but not exhaustively) to us. But at the same time the Christian believer will acknowledge that other religious systems can also contain authentic revelation. As John Hick puts it: Christians can say that God is truly to be encountered in Jesus but not only in Jesus. Jesus, he says, is *totus Deus*, that is, one who is totally expressive of God, but not *totus Dei*, that is, the exhaustive expression or revelation of God.[25] In other words, the Christian believer will also recognise that there are quasi-autonomous revelations in other religious systems, and that, so to speak, God's revelation will only be known in its fullness when all the 'revelations' to be found in the various other religions are brought together in some way and the jigsaw is completed, although we must not think that we will end up with some kind of eclectic amalgam or synthesis of religious beliefs and practices, or even that it is desirable or practicable to try to achieve such a synthesis. To make use of another very limping analogy: if we look at all the major linguistic families – Indo-European, Finno-Ugaritic, Australian etc. – we can gain some idea of the possibilities of human language better than if we simply look at one. But it is neither desirable nor practicable to attempt to establish a synthetic 'universal' language.

A more qualified version of this fourth position has been put forward in a seminal essay on Christianity and world religions written in 1961 by the great Catholic theologian Karl Rahner. Rahner emphasises that while for the Christian, Christ is the 'final, unsurpassable, irreversible' historical realisation of what God is doing in history, at the same time non-Christian religions can be

a positive means of gaining the right relationship to God and thus for the attaining of salvation – a means which is therefore positively included in God's plan for salvation.[26]

Thus, according to Rahner, religions such as Islam or Buddhism, which, in effect, do not accept that Christ is the sole manifestation

---

[25] In Hick and Knitter eds. *The Myth of Christian Uniqueness.*
[26] 'Christianity and the Non-Christian Religions', in *Theological Investigations*, vol. V, London, Darton, Longman and Todd, 1966, pp. 115–34.

of God or of the divine in human history, can nevertheless be positive ways of gaining 'the right relationship to God and of attaining salvation', and as such be 'positively included in God's plan for salvation'. Rahner refers to believers of good will in other religions as 'anonymous Christians', a description which has given great offence. However, as has been pointed out:

> Rahner proposed the theory of anonymous Christianity not for procla-mation to outsiders but solely for Christian consumption . . . to convince Christians that God's saving presence is greater than humans and the Church.[27]

It is this latter idea which is centrally important in Rahner's thought. (Rahner relates that he was once asked by the Japanese philosopher Nishitani, 'What would you say if I were to treat you as an anonymous Zen Buddhist?' Rahner's response was that Nishitani should in fact treat him in exactly this way.[28])

A similar position is taken up by Raimundo Pannikar (at least in his earlier writings) who, while maintaining the paradigmatic status of Christ, at the same time acknowledges that other world religions have their own positive value as quasi-autonomous 'revelations' of the divine.[29] 'However, this is not an exclusively Christian position, since in certain forms of Buddhism a similar stance is adopted. Thus, in the particular tradition of Buddhism to which the Dalai Lama belongs (the dGe lugs – 'Geluk' – tradition founded in the fourteenth century) it is emphasised that Buddhism does not make exclusivist claims for its corpus of religious truth and that other religious ways have their own value. As it has been put:

> Just as the Buddha taught many teachings within Buddhism to suit those at different levels, it is appropriate for a Buddhist (and may be true) to see other religions as teachings of the compassionate Buddha for those in different circumstances and situations. But at the same time this tradition maintains that the final truth is that of Madhyamaka Buddhism as understood by the Geluk tradition.[30]

---

[27] On the development of Rahner's thought on world religions see the remarkable article by Joseph H. Wong, 'Anonymous Christians: Karl Rahner's Pneuma-Christocentrism and an East–West Dialogue', *Theological Studies*, 55, 1994, 609–37.

[28] 'The One Christ and the Universality of Salvation', in *Theological Investigations*, vol. 16, 1979, p. 219.

[29] 'Religious Pluralism; The Metaphysical Challenge', in Leroy S. Rouner ed., *Religious Pluralism*, Boston, 1984.

This tradition has a well-defined philosophical methodology which emphasises the importance of analytic rationality and rejects any kind of epistemological relativism or pluralism. In consequence:

> In terms of reasoning to find the ultimate truth, if carried out correctly and without bias the Dalai Lama holds as himself and Buddhist, in common with all dGe lugs practitioners, that only Buddhism will be found to make final sense.[31]

From one point of view, this position could be seen to be an extended version of the third position looked at above, namely that, while other religions may have their own quasi-autonomous value as authentic 'revelations', their value is to be measured finally in terms of the paradigmatic or 'standard' or model religion, whatever that may be (Christianity, Buddhism, Islam etc.) However, the fourth position makes use of the important notion of the 'development' of what I have called the original revelation of a religion. We saw in the discussion of ecumenism between the Christian churches that certain values may be developed in one form of Christianity and not in others. So also in the wider sphere of the world religions, certain authentic religious values that are implicitly in the Christian revelation, but which have not been actually developed or actualised within the historical forms of Christianity, may be manifested or expressed in Hinduism or Buddhism or Islam etc. And, of course, the same is true of the other religions *vis-à-vis* Christianity and the other world religions.

A PLURALISM OF AUTONOMOUS AND INCOMMENSURABLE REVELATIONS

Some Christian thinkers have attempted to meet the difficulties of the third position, namely that it does not sufficiently recognise the autonomy of other religions, by taking up a much more radical position which sees Christianity as simply one among a number of competing, completely autonomous and quasi-incommensurable 'revelations'. Thus John Hick argues for a theocentric religious perspective that would replace our present Christocentric view:

---

[30] Paul Williams, 'Some Dimensions of the Recent Work of Raimundo Pannikar; A Buddhist Perspective', *Religious Studies*, 27, 1991, 520.   [31] Ibid.

Christianity would then become one approach to God among a number of other, equally valid, approaches.[32] Again, in a recent essay, Pannikar argues that, because Reality transcends human consciousness, there can be multiple or plural human approaches to Reality in the world religions. They are, as it were, different windows onto Reality, each autonomously valid in their own way. The appropriate response to this realisation is what Pannikar calls 'cosmic confidence', which enables us to be sure that what we do not fully understand, and which may appear to be contradictory and unintelligible, will ultimately prove not to be so. There is, Pannikar claims, an 'invisible harmony' among the many different and apparently discordant religious revelations.[33]

In Pannikar's later work, he distinguishes between 'Christ' as a universal principle – the most powerful symbol of the Absolute Reality Pannikar calls 'the Mystery' – and Jesus, an historical figure who expresses, or is an epiphany of, the Christ symbol. According to Pannikar, while it is correct to say that 'Jesus is Christ', that is a particular expression of the universal Christ, it is not correct to say that 'Christ is Jesus'. After all, the eternal Christ, or the Second Person of the Trinity, or the Logos, existed before the historical Jesus. As we have noted, for Pannikar, Jesus is a special epiphany of the Christ principle, but the latter is also expressed in other religious figures and also has other names such as Rama or Krishna. Each name is an expression of the same Mystery and each manifests an unknown dimension of Christ.[34]

An even more radical version of this pluralist theory has been proposed by the remarkable French Islamicist, Henry Corbin, for whom pluralism and diversity is a necessary and inescapable feature of religion or 'the divine'. When the *one* transcendent Reality is manifested in the world of human history, it cannot but be manifested or revealed, Corbin argues, as *many*, that is as diverse

---

[32] See John Hick, 'Jesus and the World Religions', in J. Hick ed., *The Myth of God Incarnate*, London, SCM Press, 1977.

[33] 'The Invisible Harmony: a Universal Theory of Religion or a Cosmic Confidence in Reality', in L. Swidler ed., *Towards a Universal Theology*, New York, Orbis, 1988.

[34] R. Pannikar, *The Unknown Christ of Hinduism: Towards an Ecumenical Christophany*, New York, Orbis, 1981. See also the work of John B. Cobb, *Christ in a Pluralistic Age*, Philadelphia, Westminister Press, 1975, which distinguishes between Christ as the Logos or the transcendent principle of 'creative transformation' in the world, and Jesus as the perfect incarnation of the Logos and the supreme embodiment of humanity.

and plural. Drawing on the great Neoplatonist Proclus, the twelfth-century Persian Zoroastrian thinker, Sohrawardi, and the twelfth-century Spanish Muslim thinker, Ibn Al'Arabi, Corbin sums up this idea in the striking phrase *Non Deus nisi Dii* ('There is no God without Gods'). 'It is', he says, 'in the very nature of the *Theotes* (*deitas abscondita*) to be revealed and made manifest by the plurality of its theophanies, in an unlimited number of theophanic forms'.[35]

There is a strong connection here with the Neoplatonic doctrine that the transcendent One is necessarily refracted into many 'eternal forms' which are in turn expressed in a multiplicity of 'sensible forms' as they come to be manifested in the world of space and time and materiality.[36] Corbin argues that we must resist the temptation to see the different theophanies as partial or fragmentary. In one sense they are partial as compared with the hidden divinity of which they are manifestations, but in another sense they are not, since the fullness of *Theotes* is in each.

The uniquely Divine aspires to be revealed and can only be revealed in multiple theophanies. Each one is autonomous, different from the other, each quite close to being a hypostasis, yet at the same time the totality of Theotes is in each theophanic form.

Corbin claims that Jewish and Christian monotheism confuses 'the uniqueness of Divinity (*Theotes*) with a singular God (*theos*) which excludes other gods (*theoi*)' and he argues for the recognition of a pluralism of theophanic forms. This opens the way, he says, for a return of the idea of the angels (as in Proclus and also in the Jewish Cabbala).

The Angel is the Face that our God takes for us, and each of us finds his God only when he recognises that Face. The service which we can render others is to help them to encounter that Face.[37]

Corbin's extraordinary theory obviously has revolutionary implications for our concept of God or the divine and of God's

---

[35] I am grateful to David Tacey's unpublished paper 'Many Gods, Many Ways and the Sacred' for this reference to Corbin.

[36] See Pierre Hadot ed., *Plotin: Traité* 38, VI, 7. Paris, Les Editions du Cerf, 1988.

[37] 'A Letter by Henry Corbin', Preface to David L. Miller, *The New Polytheism*, Dallas, Texas, Spring Publications, 1981.

relationship with the world of human history, and above all for the Christian view of God's unique incarnation and revelation in Jesus Christ. If Corbin were right, we could contemplate the possibility of a plurality of 'incarnations' of which the incarnation of Jesus would simply be one. If the syncretist/relativist position we looked at before sees the various religious systems as different paths up the same mountain, Corbin's position almost suggests that there are a number of quite different mountains, or in other words multiple revelations.

MULTIPLE REVELATIONS: DIFFICULTIES

However, attractive as some aspects of Corbin's theory about religious diversity are – it certainly recognises the autonomy and integrity of each of the religious systems – it clearly depends upon a full-blown Neoplatonic metaphysics where the One is expressed in a multiplicity of forms. And, quite apart from the intrinsic difficulties of that metaphysical theory, there is another difficulty in that, as a specific philosophical position, it conflicts with the philosophical theories that are bound up implicitly with other religious systems. Thus, as we have seen, for both Pannikar and Corbin, religious diversity is explained, and made acceptable, on the basis of a philosophical theory which sharply distinguishes between God or Reality on the one hand and its manifestations or 'theophanies', on the other. But in many religious systems it is not possible to make such a distinction. Thus, for example, in the dGe lugs Buddhist tradition of the Dalai Lama, which is bound up with the philosophical ideas of the Madhyamaka movement in Indian Buddhism, there is no Absolute Reality and the ultimate truth is the realisation that there is no Absolute but 'emptiness'. As it has been put:

Emptiness equals absence of inherent existence, which is to say lacking ultimate existence or essence. When Madhyamika Buddhists say something is empty they mean that it does not exist from its own side apart from, say, its parts. All, absolutely all, is dependent, relative. Emptiness is the ultimate truth – that is the ultimate truth is told when we say that all things, no matter how exalted, be they Buddha, Nirvana or worms are empty of ultimate, i.e. independent, existence. The range of this even includes emptiness itself.[38]

The Buddhists of this tradition then simply reject Pannikar's and Corbin's philosophical framework which enables them to make a place for religious pluralism in the radical way described. Pannikar can only justify his theory that the many different religious systems are 'windows' looking out on Reality in terms of that philosophical theory, and the same is true of Corbin's theophanies of the 'hidden' divinity.

One might mention in passing that the same is true of Australian Aboriginal religions, which are profoundly immanentist in orientation so that it is difficult to make the distinction – common in Judaism, Christianity and Islam – between a transcendent sphere of the divine and the local manifestations of the transcendent reality. In Australian Aboriginal religions, spiritual power resides *in* the land and natural phenomena. No doubt, in the mythic stories this spiritual power (*karunpa, amawurena* as it is variously called) is deposited in the land by the Ancestor Spirits in the primordial beginning of things, but the Ancestor Spirits are not gods, nor theophanic beings, nor even exemplars of divinity. In such a religious system it is impossible to make the Neoplatonic distinction between the one divinity and the multiple theophanies – a distinction which is the basis for Pannikar's and Corbin's theoretical solutions to the problem of religious diversity.

Similar reservations have been made regarding cultural differences about the nature of time between the Hindu and Taoist cyclic view of time and the Christian linear view. In Hinduism and Taoism, the incarnation of Jesus Christ as an individual historical event is difficult to conceptualise. Christ as the universal Logos is easier to conceptualise within these cultures, and it is doubtless because of this that Pannikar and others have focussed on the 'universal Christ'.[39]

CONCLUSION

We seem, then, to be left with the fourth position outlined above as the best solution we have to the problem of religious diversity. No

---

[38] Paul Williams, 'Some Dimensions of the Recent Work of Raimundo Pannikar', p. 516.
[39] See Joseph H. Wong, 'Anonymous Christians' for a brilliant attempt to reconcile Rahner's Christological and Trinitarian position with classical Taoism.

doubt this will be far too radical for some religious believers in that,
while it allows a believer to hold that his or her religion has some
kind of paradigmatic status, it also admits that genuine religious
developments may take place in other religions. On the other hand
it will not be radical enough for other people who will see it as
denying the integrity and autonomy of other religious ways and
sanctioning some degree of religious exclusivity and 'intolerance'.
In other words, by seeing Christianity as having some essential core
of truth that Buddhism lacks, I am claiming superiority for
Christianity. And vice versa, if I claim that Buddhism is the
privileged way of enlightenment, I am claiming superiority for
Buddhism *vis-à-vis* Christianity.

Two final observations. First, the American Catholic theologian, Paul Knitter, has argued that the perspective of 'liberation
theology' can be of help in coming to grips with the issues discussed
here. The primary aim of a theological theory about religious
diversity, he says,

> should not be the 'right belief' (orthodoxy) about the uniqueness of
> Christ, but the 'right practice' (orthopraxis), with other religions, of
> furthering the Kingdom and its *soteria*.

What we should focus on is the practical value of the various
religions as 'ways of salvation'.

> Through such an ethical hermeneutics, theologians might find reason to
> affirm Christ as a unique, normative liberator – as he who unifies and
> fulfills all efforts towards a full humanity. Or, they may discover that other
> religions and religious figures offer a means and vision of liberation equal
> to that of Jesus.

This, Knitter says, 'would be a cause for Christian rejoicing.
"Anyone who is not against us is with us" (Mark 9:40)'.[40]

However, while this is, no doubt, a useful reminder of the
ultimately practical nature of all theological reflection, it does not
really offer a solution to the problem of religious diversity, since the
same kind of problems arise about the meaning of 'liberation' and
whether or not Jesus Christ's (or Buddha's or Muhammad's) life
and teaching offers a 'unique' way of human liberation. We cannot

---

[40] 'Catholic Theology of Religions at a Crossroads', *Concilium*, 183, 1983, 105–6.

really escape the need for truth or 'ortho-doxy' in the religious sphere, since, in some sense or other, the religious believer wants to hold that the revelation at the centre of his or her tradition is 'true' and not merely a useful pragmatic fiction.

A second point: in one sense the problem of religious diversity is a philosophical problem – how can we make sense of a situation where various religious systems are making what appear to be mutually contradictory truth claims? In another sense, to speak from a Christian perspective, the problem of religious diversity is a theological problem, where we are ultimately confronted with a 'mystery' which cannot be wholly explained by philosophical means, but which can be shown not to involve a formal contradiction which would render it unintelligible and unbelievable. In traditional Christian Trinitarian theology, for example, the 'mystery' is how the unicity of God is reconciled with the recognition that the Father, the Son and the Holy Spirit are properly described as 'God'. Since we cannot say that there are three Gods, nor that the Father, Son and Holy Spirit are merely three aspects of the one God, the philosophical notion of 'person' is introduced, not to *explain* the Trinity, but, in a sense, to make it clear that belief in the Trinity does not, on the one hand, involve belief in the existence of three Gods and (as Muslim critics believe) the rejection of the unicity of God, and does not, on the other hand, involve a belief that the Father, Son and Holy Spirit are mere aspects of the one God. Allowing for the moment that the theological notion of 'person' is meaningful, its function is a negative one in that it tells the believer how *not* to see the Trinity.

In the case of religious diversity, the 'mystery' is, on the one hand, the reconciliation of the truth that God wills that all human beings be saved or achieve enlightenment and that they have, in some way, access to the means of salvation or enlightenment through some mode of revelation; and, on the other hand, the truth that there is prima facie a diversity of religious revelations. We cannot *explain* in any positive sense how this reconciliation is possible, but we can, perhaps, show, on the one hand, what is *not* involved in believing that God wills that all should be offered the means of salvation or enlightenment and, on the other hand, recognition of the fact of religious diversity.

Operationally, what does all this abstruse speculation mean for the ordinary religious believer who confronts the problem of religious diversity? Let us put our reply in the form of a credo for the religious believer.

1. I believe that 'God'[41] wills that all should be saved or achieve enlightenment and that all human beings have access to the means of salvation or enlightenment through some mode of revelation.

2. I believe (as a Christian, or a Jew, or a Muslim, or a Hindu or Buddhist etc.) that my religious tradition has a privileged and paradigmatic status and that 'God' has revealed himself most completely in that tradition.

3. I believe that certain authentic religious values which are implicit or latent within my tradition, but which have not actually been developed within that tradition, may be manifested or expressed in other religious traditions.

4. I believe that there is also the possibility of authentic religious revelations, complementary to the paradigmatic revelation of my tradition but 'outside' my own tradition.

5. I believe that 'God's revelation' will only be known in its fullness when, as an ideal limit, all the 'revelations' and their 'developments' are brought together in some way.

6. I believe that religious diversity is in some sense willed by 'God' and has its own intrinsic meaning and purpose and is not merely the result of sin and ignorance.

7. I believe that respect for, openness to, and dialogue with, other religious traditions, must be part of any authentic religious tradition.

Religious believers have to work out what this credo means with regard to their own particular religion, and what kind of restructuring of belief and the institutions of belief it requires. As I mentioned above, this is a task even more radical and momentous than that which confronted the early Christian communities when they realised that the second coming of Jesus was not imminent.

[41] 'God' here is taken to mean any source of revelation or disclosure of 'the divine'.

The invention of Australian Aboriginal religion

THE ANTHROPOLOGY OF ANTHROPOLOGY

One of the most interesting trends in contemporary anthropology has been what might be called the anthropology of anthropology. This is concerned with the study of the emergence of anthropology as a discipline in the late nineteenth century, and its development in the twentieth century, as itself a socio-cultural phenomenon that can be investigated in a broadly anthropological way. Claude Lévi-Strauss remarks somewhere that the main difference between western culture and non-western cultures is that 'we' have anthropologists and 'they' do not, and there is a good deal of point to Lévi-Strauss's irony. It suggests that, just as the anthropologist is concerned to see other ways of life as cultural artefacts or constructs, so also the discipline of anthropology can be seen as a cultural construct or invention: it is an expression of 'our' way of life *vis-à-vis* other non-western ways of life. If the anthropologist is concerned 'to see culture and its norms – beauty, truth, reality – as artificial arrangements susceptible to detached analysis and comparison with other possible dispositions',[1] the sub-culture of western anthropology itself can be seen as an artificial arrangement susceptible to detached analysis and comparison with other possible dispositions. The anthropological torch can, so to speak, be turned upon anthropology and anthropologists themselves.

A number of contemporary scholars – Clifford Geertz, Paul Rabinow, James Clifford and others[2] – have tried to show how the

---

[1] James Clifford, *The Predicament of Culture*, Cambridge, Mass., Harvard University Press, 1988, p. 119.
[2] See Clifford, ibid.; Clifford Geertz, *Local Knowledge: Further Essays in Interpretive Anthropology*, New York, Basic Books, 1983.

methodology and styles and literary forms and devices of nine-
teenth- and twentieth-century anthropology are all cultural artefacts or 'constructions', and how the anthropological understanding of so-called 'primitive' or pre-literate cultures has always been a
matter of negotiation (sometimes tacit, sometimes explicit) between
the culture represented by anthropologists and the cultures of their
subjects. In other words, what the anthropologist tells us about the
Sudanese Nuer or the African Dogon or the Australian Warlpiri is
the result of an exchange between a representative of a sub-culture
of western culture (the anthropologist) and people from those other
cultures. It is not just a matter of direct and unmediated 'observation' (of a positivistic kind) by the anthropologist of his or her
subjects: rather, the anthropologist is himself or herself part of the
equation. The anthropologist Evans-Pritchard is observing what
the Nuer allow him to observe and he is also observing a group of
people who have been changed by the fact that they have a person
from another culture among them who is 'observing' them in a
'detached' way. As James Clifford puts it in his excellent book, *The
Predicament of Culture*,[3] Griaule's celebrated studies of the African
Dogon tell us as much about Griaule and his culture between 1930
and 1960 as they tell us about the Dogon (just as some have claimed
that Freud's 'cases' tell us as much about Freud himself, and the
medical sub-culture he represented, as about his unfortunate
subjects).

For some of the meta-anthropologists, this is a much more
radical thesis than the obvious point that we inevitably approach
other cultures with our own set of cultural preconceptions and
prejudices which we must as far as possible set aside if we are to
understand other cultures 'in their own terms'. That allows the
possibility, even if it is merely an ideal possibility, of gradually
overcoming our cultural myopia so that we may eventually
understand other cultures with some kind of 'objectivity'.
Rabinow's and Clifford's argument, however, is that this is
impossible, since every anthropological understanding is culturally
negotiated: it is an essay in intercultural exchange. Just as Kant
argued that we cannot know the world of sense perception directly,

---

[3] Ibid.

but only as mediated through the 'categories' of the understanding, so we can know other cultures only in a mediated way through our own cultural and sub-cultural categories. Thus Clifford, analysing Michel Leiris' essay *The African Negroes and the Arts of Carving and Sculpture*, remarks that Leiris

writes as a westerner perceiving similarities among the diverse sculptures of Africa and even presenting them as expressions of 'civilisation' while understanding these ensembles to be in a sense optical illusions. The apparent unity of black art inheres only in a perception of the common ways in which they differ from those to which a European is accustomed.[4]

We shall discuss later whether this kind of anthropological Kantianism excludes any 'objectivity' in our observations of other cultures, and whether it is subject to the same kind of objections as Kant's own theory of knowledge. For the moment we can remain content with a looser and less radical version of the theory to the effect that western anthropological observations of non-western cultures are to some extent 'constructed', or 'invented', or are 'artefacts' of the anthropological method itself (or of certain conceptions of the anthropological method). In this view, we can understand other cultures and their belief systems and achieve a degree of objectivity about them, although our understanding is primarily of an oblique and analogous kind.

AUSTRALIAN ABORIGINAL PREHISTORY AND CULTURE

Since we are concerned here with the way in which anthropological approaches to Australian Aboriginal cultures have shaped the picture that we now have of those cultures and their religions, it may be helpful if we begin with a brief introduction to the essential features of Australian Aboriginal prehistory and culture. Though the archaeological evidence is very sparse, there is a strong supposition that the Australian Aborigines have been in Australia for more than 50,000 years. It has been surmised that the remote ancestors of the Aborigines came from South Asia either through Timor and thence to the Kimberley region in the north of Western Australia, or through New Guinea to Arnhem Land at a time when

---

[4] Ibid. p. 89.

the sea-level was much lower than it is now. Fifty thousand years ago Australia was joined to Papua New Guinea in the north-east, and access by land and short water crossings via the north-west islands between Indonesia and Australia was comparatively simple. At that time also, in the south, Tasmania was joined by land to the Australian mainland.[5]

The Aborigines brought with them stone tools and implements and a knowledge of fire (later used extensively in 'farming' practices) and they spread out in small groups right through the vast continent, occupying roughly the same area as the United States of America. After this diffusion, deep linguistic and cultural and religious differences developed in the various regions. As has been said:

That there existed no single Aboriginal way is reflected in the regionally diverse archaeological remains and the technological and aesthetic variation reflected in material culture and art forms.[6]

With the Australian Aborigines we are not, then, dealing with a unitary people, or a nation with a unitary culture or way of life: 'Australian Aboriginal' is an umbrella term covering very deep and wide differences.

At all events, it is known that by 20,000 years ago Aboriginal groups had settled as far apart as Arnhem Land in the north and the caves of south-west Tasmania in the south. Among the few pieces of evidence that have been discovered is a male burial, with red ochre dusted over the skeleton, dating from 30,000 years ago, and the remains of a cremated female from some 26,000 years ago. Both appear to have been religious ritual burials.

What evidence there is suggests that there were perhaps two distinct waves of Aboriginal migrants into Australia. The first had a

[5] On the prehistory of Australia see D. J. Mulvaney, *The Prehistory of Australia*, Ringwood, Penguin Books, 1978, and Josephine Flood, *Archaeology of the Dreamtime: The Story of Prehistoric Australia and the People*, Sydney, Collins, 1983. See also D. J. Mulvaney, 'A Sense of Making History: Australian Aboriginal Studies 1961–1986, in *Australian Aborginal Studies*, 2, 1986, 48–56.

[6] Mulvaney, 'A Sense of Making History', 54. See also Jeremy Beckett, ed., *Past and Present: The Construction of Aboriginality*, Aboriginal Studies Press, Canberra, 1988, and Steven Thiele, ed., 'Reconsidering Aboriginality', *The Australian Journal of Anthropology*, Special Issue 2, 1991, 2:2; see especially Kenneth Maddock, 'Metamorphosing the Sacred in Australia', 213–31, and Iain Davidson, 'Archaeologists and Aborigines', 247–58.

'robust' skeletal form, and may have entered Australia some 70,000 years ago; the second had a 'gracile' or slender form and probably entered 50,000 years ago. Again, it seems that these two groups may have had different burial customs and a different stone technology. It has also been suggested that, while the robust people originated in Indonesia, the gracile people originated in southern China.

About 6000 years ago, the distinct robust and gracile types seem to have disappeared, and prototypes of the modern Australian Aborigine appeared on the scene. We do not know whether the robust and gracile types were transformed into the modern type or whether the latter replaced them. However, we need to remember that all this is largely surmise and speculation, and we have very little hard evidence about the first Australians. It seems, however, to be a reasonable supposition that they were ancestors of the modern Aborigines.

For many years it was thought that by the beginning of European occupation and settlement in 1788 the total number of Aborigines was no more than 300,000. However, recent research has indicated that Aboriginal settlement was more extensive and denser than previously thought and it is now surmised that the Aboriginal population in 1788 was at least 750,000. (The size of the present Aboriginal population is about 180,000.)

Those 750,000 Australian Aborigines were divided into 500 distinct groups using more than 200 distinct languages. Some languages belong to the same 'family', just as Sanskrit, Latin and English and German belong to the Indo-European language family. But the various Aboriginal languages are as distinct as the latter and are not merely dialects. A Pintubi speaker from central Australia will not be able to understand a Pitjantjatjara speaker from the western desert region and neither will be able to understand a Yolngu speaker from Arnhem land. Many Aboriginal languages have died out (it has been estimated that 150 are extinct and that another 100 are on the way to extinction), but the main extant languages, such as Warlpiri, Pintubi, Aranda, Pitjatjatjara, Yolngu etc., are alive and vigorous.[7]

---

[7] The best account of Australian Aboriginal Languages is that by R. M. W. Dixon, *Languages of Australia*, Cambridge University Press, 1980.

In the same way as the various Aboriginal languages constituted a linguistic 'family', the 500 Aboriginal social groupings also had certain structural similarities. The centre of the Australian Aborigines' economic, social, cultural and religious interest was the relatively small group of between 100 and 300 people to which they belonged. Each group (though there were regional similarities) had its own language, inhabited a defined territory given by an Ancestor Spirit, followed its own religious 'law' laid down by the Ancestor Spirit, and had its own distinctive form of artistic expression. These groups were not 'tribes' in the usual sense of that word since Aboriginal social organisation and relationship to territory was much more flexible than that of ordinary tribal societies.[8] It is worthwhile remarking that the various groups had no sense of belonging to a common Australia-wide pan-Aboriginal nation.

The groups were usually divided into two classes or (to use the anthropological term) 'moieties'. In the case of the Arnhem Land Yolngu people these were called the Dhuwa and the Yirritja. These divisions or moieties are exogamous, that is, those in the one moiety must 'marry out' or choose a wife or husband in the other moiety. Thus, among the Yolngu people, a man belonging to a clan of the Dhuwa moiety must marry a wife belonging to a clan of the Yirritja moiety, and vice versa.

These divisions apply not only to human beings, but also to the structure of the universe itself.

For the Yolngu the Ancestral beings who created the land, the winds that blow across it from different directions and the ochres that lie beneath the soil are either Dhuwa or Yirritja, never both.[9]

Just as social classes ensure that every human being has a defined place and role, so the division of natural phenomena into classes ensures that everything in the world has its specific place and role. It has been said that the Australian Aborigines have a 'passion for order' and the classification system is clearly an important part of this.[10]

See the introduction to N. Peterson ed., *Tribes and Boundaries in Australia*, Canberra, Australian Institute of Aboriginal Studies, 1976.

Howard Morphy, *Journey to the Crocodile's Nest*, Canberra, Australian Institute of Aboriginal Studies, 1984, p. 7.

See Kenneth Maddock, *The Australian Aborigines: A Portrait of Their Society*, Ringwood, Penguin Books, 1982, p. 96.

The Australian Aborigines were formerly categorised as 'nomads', that is people who travel around a territory without any fixed base, hunting animals and fish and gathering fruit, berries, seeds, roots and so on, and generally living at a bare subsistence level. However, the Aborigines are not really nomadic, since they travel around a fixed and well-defined territory and many groups have quasi-permanent bases. Again, while it is too much to say that the Aborigines enjoyed a life of what has been called 'Stone Age original affluence', most of the Aboriginal groups lived well above bare subsistence level. Indeed, considerably more time was spent by Aboriginal groups in social and religious activities than in broadly economic and material pursuits.

It is also not entirely correct to say that the Australian Aborigines were 'hunter gatherers' along with other food-collecting groups such as the Eskimos, the African Bushmen etc., as distinct from food-producing societies where people lived a stable and sedentary life in one place and engaged in gardening and agriculture. The Aborigines used fire extensively to modify their environment, and some groups also used weirs and dams and were as much concerned with forms of food-production as with food-collection.[11]

It has been said, misleadingly, that the Australian Aborigines are a 'people without politics'. However, while the Aboriginal groups do not have political structures of the kind that characterise European societies, they do have their own kind of diffuse and decentralised political order and their own dispute-resolution procedures. The kind of 'ordered anarchy' which is typical of Australian Aboriginal groups is powerfully supported by the kinship and class systems which define each person's rights and duties and privileges and which force the various sub-groups into interdependence.[12]

ANTHROPOLOGICAL APPROACHES

There have been a number of quite different anthropological approaches to Australian Aboriginal cultures which have shaped

---

[11] See the essays in N. M. Williams and E. S. Hunn eds. *Resource Managers: North American and Australian Hunter Gatherers*, Canberra, Australian Institute of Aboriginal Studies, 1982.

[12] See Nancy M. Williams, 'On Aboriginal Decision-Making', in D. E. Barwick ed., *Metaphors of Interpretation*, Canberra, Australian National University Press, 1985.

the picture that we now have of those cultures and their religions. First, the pervasive evolutionism of the late nineteenth century and the early twentieth century demanded, so to speak, that there be a pre-religious and pre-scientific stage in the development of human consciousness. Consequently, when the Australian Aborigines first appeared on the scholarly scene in the nineteenth century, through the works of Howitt and Fison and Spencer and Gillen, they were seized upon to fill the role that Robertson Smith and Tylor and other English cultural evolutionists had decreed must exist. The Australian Aborigines were seen as the paradigmatic 'primitives' in a way in which African and other 'primitives' were not, and it was assumed that they were not capable of religion, or up to the religious stage in human development, but remained fixed at the pre-religious level of 'magic' (that convenient nineteenth century *omnium gatherum* concept). As Sir James Frazer (of *The Golden Bough*) wrote:

Among the aborigines of Australia, the rudest savages as to whom we possess accurate information, magic is universally practised, whereas religion, in the sense of a propitiation of the higher powers, seems to be unknown.[13]

FRAZER AND BALDWIN SPENCER

Frazer had a powerful influence upon the early observers of Australian religion and for the most part they dutifully saw what Frazer told them to see. Baldwin Spencer, for example, was a sympathetic and acute observer, and it is almost tragic to see how, under Frazer's spell, he so often missed the point of what was before his eyes. Later on, A. P. Elkin, one of the significant figures in early Australian anthropology (and one of the very few with any philosophical interests and inclinations),[14] was to say that in the 1920s he had been convinced,

looking at the material written by Strehlow's father and by Spencer and Gillen, that they were dealing with religious ceremonies: but Sir James Frazer's view that they were only magic rites was difficult to counteract.[15]

Frazer's influence upon Baldwin Spencer is marvellously described

---

[13] *The Golden Bough*, abridged edition, London, Macmillan, 1960, p. 72.
[14] See A. P. Elkin, 'Elements of Australian Aboriginal Philosophy', *Oceania*, 40, 1969, 40.
[15] A. P. Elkin, in Helen Shields ed., *Australian Aboriginal Studies*, Melbourne, Oxford University Press, 1963, p. 252.

by D. J. Mulvaney in his magisterial biography of Spencer[16] and it is worthwhile citing him at length:

Spencer was familiar with Frazer's *The Golden Bough* before its author first wrote to him. Its thesis that society passed from a state of magical practices to religious beliefs and eventually to scientific truth appealed to him. Before Frazer first contacted him he had inferred that Aboriginal society belonged to the lowest cognitive level and that totemic ceremonials were magical increase rites intended to ensure the perpetuation of a particular species. Frazer's mentor, Robertson Smith, had predicted that such rites would be found to be practised by a contemporary society. Spencer obliged by reasoning that the ceremonies which he witnessed in Alice Springs were elemental sacramental feasts. This idea first occurred to him in mid-1897, whereupon he sought further details from Gillen, who replied with respect: 'the blackfellow eating the flesh and blood of his totem in the same spirit that the Christian takes the sacrament is a thing that would never have dawned upon my muddy mind'. The fact was, however, that under the subsequent tutelage of Frazer, Spencer adopted a terminology from which creative 'religious' actions were excluded. In Frazer's company at the Anthropological Institute in London a year later, Spencer announced that 'Mr Frazer would now prefer to designate (Arunta totemism) as magical rather than religious.' So 'magical' it remained with all the intellectual denigration of the Aboriginal mind implied by that term. There is no index entry under 'religion' in any of Spencer's books, although there are numerous under 'totem' and 'magic'. 'The natives have nothing whatever in the way of simple, pure religion', he assured Frazer later.[17]

It is worth remarking that 'magic', as applied to Aboriginal beliefs and practices, was an ambivalent term in that it was interpreted both as a pre-religious and pre-scientific mode of consciousness and also as a kind of 'fallen' or debased kind of religious consciousness. As it has been put: the Aborigines were viewed as being 'either too archaic in the social sense or too debased in the moral sense to have veritable religion'.[18]

DURKHEIM

A second anthropological perspective which has powerfully shaped our view of Australian Aboriginal religion derived from Emile

---

[16] D. J. Mulvaney, *'So Much That is New' – Baldwin Spencer, 1860– 1929: A Biography*, Melbourne, Melbourne University Press, 1985.   [17] Ibid., pp. 391–2.

[18] W. E. H. Stanner, 'Religion, Totemism and Symbolism', in R. M. and C. H. Berndt eds., *Aboriginal Man in Australia*, Sydney, Angus and Robertson, 1965, p. 209.

Durkheim's great work, *The Elementary Forms of the Religious Life: The Totemic System in Australia*, which appeared in 1912. Durkheim acknowledged that Australian Aboriginal religion was authentically 'religion', but also that it was the most 'elementary' form of religion in which one could discern the essence of religious life in its clearest and simplest form. (For Durkheim, Australian Aboriginal religion was 'elementary' in the sense in which the chemical elements were 'elementary'.) Durkheim had already formed his views on culture and religion, and his theory demanded that there be a most elementary form of social life with the most elementary form of religion – a situation which would make it clear that society and religion were one, since the prime function of religion was to reinforce the social bond. Unfortunately for the Australian Aborigines, fieldwork evidence about them (from Howitt, Baldwin Spencer, Gillen and others) came on stream just at the crucial time, and Durkheim seized upon that evidence as proof of his theory of religion and society. (As someone has cynically remarked: if the Australian Aborigines had not existed it would have been necessary for Durkheim to invent them since they – or some such group of 'primitives' – were required to exist by the logic of his theory.)

Durkheim closely studied the ethnographic material from Australia – Spencer's and Gillen's *The Native Tribes of Central Australia*, Howitt's *The Native Tribes of South Eastern Australia* and Pastor Strehlow's study of the Aranda. Marcel Mauss, one of Durkheim's followers, described Spencer's and Gillen's work as

one of the most important books of ethnography and descriptive sociology of which we know . . . the picture they give us of social and religious organisation is one of the most complete with which anthropology has provided us.[19]

At all events, after Durkheim, the Australian Aborigines were henceforth seen as exemplars of the most elementary form of social organisation with the most elementary religious beliefs and practices. It has taken almost eighty years for the Australian Aborigines to escape from that typification.

It is all too easy to pass from the neutral evolutionary sense of the

---

[19] Cited in S. Lukes, *Emile Durkheim – His Life and Work: A Historical and Critical Study*, Harmondsworth, Penguin, 1975, p. 452.

'elementary' as meaning 'simple' or relatively 'non-complex' to a pejorative evaluative sense. Thus Durkheim's view of the elementary character of Australian Aboriginal religion was interpreted by some anthropologists as meaning that it was not merely simple, but simple-minded (notwithstanding the extraordinary complexity of Aboriginal social life and of Aboriginal languages). Australian Aboriginal thought came to be seen as being 'pre-logical' in Lévy-Bruhl's sense in his characterisation of *la mentalité primitive*.[20] This idea, we shall see, resurfaces in the anthropological construction of the central phenomenon of Australian Aboriginal religions, now unhappily called 'the Dreaming'. Durkheim's approach also, of course, supported the theory of totemism, one of the most extraordinary theoretical inventions of later nineteenth- and early twentieth-century anthropology, so that Australian Aboriginal religions came to be seen as centred on totemic figures incarnating the social consciousness of the clan.

The story of the theory of totemism in early Australian Aboriginal anthropology is a very confused one. Defined in the most general sense as 'the use of the environment as a semiotic resource'[21] totemism is pervasive in Aboriginal society linking personal, kin, clan and fundamental cosmic realities. But these links are shifting and fluid and not systematic or fixed or deterministic. As Lévi-Strauss argued in 1964,[22] totemism as a unitary phenomenon does not exist, and the use of the category of totemism imposed a false appearance of order and system on the phenomena of Aboriginal cultures and religions. Using Lévi-Strauss' ideas, Peter Worsley[23] showed that, while each Groote Eylandt clan has a set of totems, there is no overarching system of totemic symbolism between the clans. As Worsley says,

the appearance of compendious systematisation can be 'substantiated' only by selective and unscientific concentration upon the more systematic

[20] Lucien Lévy-Bruhl, *Les Fonctions mentales dans les sociétés inférieures*, English translation, *How Natives Think*, London, 1926.
[21] Howard Morphy, 'The Resurrection of the Hydra: Twenty Five Years of Research on Aboriginal Religion', in R. M. Berndt ed., *Social Anthropology and Australian Aboriginal Studies*, Canberra, Aboriginal Studies Press, 1988, p. 249.
[22] *Totemism*, London, Merlin Press, 1964.
[23] 'Groote Eylandt Totemism and "Le Totemisme aujourd'hui"', in E. R. Leach ed., *The Structural Study of Myth and Totemism*, London, Tavistock, 1967.

parts of the totemic compendium to the exclusion of all the contingent parts.[24]

Largely due to the sceptical views of Stanner, Worsley and others, the use of the concept of totemism (so widespread in late nineteenth and early twentieth-century Aboriginal anthropology) has not had the untoward effects – overemphasising the appearance of 'compendious systematisation' – it might have had on anthropological approaches to Australian Aboriginal religion.[25]

A third important anthropological approach which helped form a perspective on Australian Aboriginal culture and religion derived from the work of A. R. Radcliffe-Brown. Radcliffe-Brown was a pupil of W. H. R. Rivers (1864–1922), one of the founding fathers of modern British anthropology, who in his quest to make anthropology into a strict and rigorous 'science', fixed upon the study of kinship relations and social organisation as the primary object of the new discipline. The focus of the new Cambridge school was on social structure, since this was an aspect of primitive culture which seemed to best lend itself to 'hard' scientific investigation. Radcliffe-Brown developed and refined Rivers' seminal idea, and, during his term as foundation professor of anthropology at the University of Sydney between 1926 and 1931, he bequeathed it to subsequent Australian anthropology. For Radcliffe-Brown and his school, it was the structure of Australian Aboriginal society that was of primary importance, and religion was seen largely as a secondary phenomenon, so that the mystical and mythical dimensions of Australian Aboriginal life were relegated to a subordinate place.[26]

Again, the radically ahistorical approach that Radcliffe-Brown and his followers introduced into anthropology de-emphasised cultural and religious change and development and made it appear that Aboriginal society, and Aboriginal religions in particular, were wholly static and conservative and 'timeless'. As Rosaldo and other

---

[24] Ibid., p. 151
[25] See W. E. H. Stanner, 'Religion, Totemism and Symbolism', in R. M. and C. H. Berndt eds., *Aboriginal Man in Australia*, pp. 207–37. For a perceptive account of the career of the concept of totemism in Australian Aboriginal anthropology see Howard Morphy, 'The Resurrection of the Hydra', pp. 244–9.
[26] On Radcliffe-Brown see Ian Langham's perceptive study, *The Making of British Social Anthropology*, Dordrecht, Reidel, 1981.

recent anthropological scholars have argued, this view of the 'timeless primitive' living in a 'timeless land' is very largely an artefact of ethnographic method rather than a reflection of the reality of primitive societies. If one adopts a synchronic ahistorical approach and looks at socio-cultural structures as though they existed in a timeless present, then one will, of course, see them as unchanging and ahistorical.[27]

Before Radcliffe-Brown, Baldwin Spencer also shared the prejudice that Australian Aboriginal culture was totally conservative and unchanging. Indeed, this was, for Baldwin Spencer, so much of the essence of Aboriginal society that any change introduced from without was bound to be destructive. While change was associated with 'progress' and human betterment in western culture, it inevitably meant degeneration in Australian Aboriginal culture. As Mulvaney notes: for Spencer

Aboriginal culture was in a sense monolithic, with its social and belief systems unchanged since time immemorial. Cultural transformations came from external pressures and not from any internal dynamism; such outside influences 'contained' the original system. While the doctrine of progress and utilitarianism ensured an ever happier future for European mankind, it was 'degeneration' when Aboriginal society accepted new ideas or customs.[28]

At all events, there is good reason to think that the anthropological myth that the Australian Aborigines lived in a 'timeless land' and that their culture and religion was similarly timeless and unchanging, is no more than 'an artifact of the ethnographic method'. Thus, writing of the Mardudjara people, Robert Tonkinson notes four sources of change and innovation in Aboriginal religion: 'the diffusion of new rituals, songlines, and objects between groups', 'ritual innovations at the local level', 'discoveries of sacred objects' and 'the exploitation of myth's inherent flexibility'.[29] Thus, with respect to the diffusion of new rituals and songs, Tonkinson notes

---

[27] R. Rosaldo, *Ilongot Headhunting 1883–1974: A Study of Society in History*, Palo Alto, Stanford University Press, 1980.   [28] *'So Much That is New'*, p. 212.
[29] Robert Tonkinson, *The Mardudjara Aborigines*, New York, Holt, Rinehart and Winston, 1978, p. 113. See also Max Charlesworth, Howard Morphy, Diane Bell, Kenneth Maddock eds., *Religion in Aboriginal Australia: An Anthology*, St Lucia, University of Queensland Press, 1984: see especially Part 4, Change in Aboriginal Religion. This section of the text above is based upon Part 4.

that, at the 'big meetings', when groups come together 'in emulation of the Dreamtime beings who instituted and exchanged rituals and objects on many occasions when their paths crossed', a great deal of religious 'exchange' and barter takes place. Rituals and songs are 'owned' by particular groups and they may be exchanged or traded with other groups and modified by the latter so that they become their property.[30]

Second, innovation in religious rituals may occur through dream-spirit 'journeys'. In dreams, rituals and other religious 'busines', new truths may be revealed to individual Aborigines, both men and women, by the powers of the Dreaming. These 'private revelations' must fit into the given religious structures, nevertheless they do provide a source of religious novelty. Innovation can also take place through the creation of new totemic songs. Thus, speaking of Groote Eylandt totemism, Worsley has this to say:

There is an important personal element in totemic innovation. This also takes the form of innovation via aesthetic creation. One single man has personally produced more new 'totemic' songs than the rest of the tribe put together, including new songs relating to military forces on Groote Eylandt and in the Second World War ('Army'), a song about 'Airbase' and a song about 'Catalina' flying boats. He likes singing and though he belongs to a clan with only one other adult married male member, he has contributed vastly and disproportionately to the totemic repertoire of the Groote Eylandters.[31]

Third, change in Aboriginal religions can take place through the discovery of sacred objects left by the Dreamtime beings. Once again, information about such objects is effected through dreams in which Aborigines claim they have met spirit beings who have described the location of objects left behind by the Dreaming ancestors. The implication of this is that the 'deposit of revelation' is not definitively completed or closed for Aborigines, since traces of the activities of the Dreamtime heroes may still be brought to life.

Fourth, religious change may be brought about through myths

---

[30] Tonkinson, *The Mardudjara Aborigines*, p. 113.

[31] Peter Worsley, 'Groote Eylandt Totemism and "le totemisme aujourd'hui"', in *Sociological Theory and Philosophical Analysis*, London, Macmillan, 1970.

which, because of their generality and schematic character, allow a wide range of different interpretations, and which may be extended and enlarged to a new and different geographical location or to a different people. Thus, Ngaawayil myths and rites concerned with the rainmaking beings were adopted, and adapted, by the Mardudjara people who amplified the myths 'to incorporate the appearance of the rainmakers in Mardudjara country and to add details of their activities there, including meetings with local beings'.[32]

A similar process has occurred with respect to Aboriginal musical activity. At first sight, learning the traditional songs by rote seems to leave almost no place for creativity on the part of performers. But, in fact, there is a great deal of concealed or surreptitious creativity. As the American linguist Ken Hale has written of the Warlpiri:

> The room for creativity is inherent in the complementary doctrine according to which young adult learners must acquire even the most difficult or 'tricky' poetic chants on the basis of evidence of the most elementary sort. In effect, one does not really learn the songs by rote: rather, one re-creates them on the basis of the evidence made available in choral singing and associated (often piecemeal) mythological narrative.[33]

Despite the prejudice of the early anthropologists that Australian Aboriginal cultures and religions were 'timeless' and unchanging, there is now a great deal of evidence that there has always been, within the framework or 'canon' provided by the foundation charter of the Dreaming, a great deal of innovation and change and reinterpretation and creative adaptation in Australian religions. No doubt, Aboriginal religious rhetoric lays great stress on the role of the Ancestor Spirits and one is sometimes given the impression that Aboriginal religions are 'fundamentalist' in orientation where the Law, laid down by the Ancestor Spirits 'at the beginning of things', has to be understood literally and observed with scupulous fidelity. But one must distinguish here between the public rhetoric of Aborigines, which gives the impression that

---

[32] Tonkinson, *The Mardudjara Aborigines*, p. 113.
[33] Cited in Paul Carter, *The Lie of the Land*, London, Faber and Faber, 1996, p. 104. See K. Hale, 'Remarks on Creativity in Aboriginal Verse', in J. C. Kassler and J. Stubington eds., *Problems and Solutions*, St Lucia, University of Queensland Press, 1984.

Aboriginal religion is essentially devoted to the faithful replication of the primordial design laid down by the Ancestor Spirits, and the reality of actual Aboriginal life and practice where there is a continual process of development and creative invention.[34]

Finally, to return to Radcliffe-Brown, one might also mention that his determination to make anthropology into a 'hard' and rigorous science meant that he was suspicious of any philosophical or comparativist perspective. This suspicion has continued in subsequent Australian Aboriginal anthropology, and there have been very few philosophical or comparative religion studies, although Stanner's early essays, 'On Aboriginal Religion' (1959–61), Elkin's essay, 'Elements of Australian Aboriginal Philosophy' (1969) and Mircea Eliade's work, *Australian Religions: An Introduction* (1973),[35] are notable exceptions. More recently, David Turner's *Life Before Genesis* (1985), and Tony Swain's *A Place for Strangers: Towards a History of Australian Aboriginal Being* (1993) are extremely interesting, if controversial, attempts to set the study of Australian Aboriginal religion within wider philosophical and theological perspectives.[36]

WOMEN'S AND MEN'S RELIGIOUS 'BUSINESS'

The way in which Australian Aboriginal religion has been understood by anthropologists has also been influenced by the fact that most of the early anthropologists were men whose only informants were male Aborigines. Given the social and religious structure of Aboriginal societies, it was impossible for a male to discuss 'religious business' with Aboriginal women. As a consequence, the whole area of women's religion, and its distinct but complementary function *vis-à-vis* male religion, has until recently been largely left out of account. (One must admit, however, that

[34] As one of Morphy's Yolngu informants put it: 'We are always running to catch up with what has gone before.' Morphy, 'The Resurrection of the Hydra', p. 249.

[35] W. E. H. Stanner, 'On Aboriginal Religion', *Oceania*, 30 (2, 4) 1959; 31 (2, 4) 1960; 32 (2, 4) 1961. M. Eliade, *Australian Religions: An Introduction*, Ithaca, Cornell University Press, 1973. Eliade's work is based upon material available before 1960 and is very much limited by this fact.

[36] David Turner, *Life Before Genesis: A Conclusion*, New York, Peter Lang, 1985. Tony Swain, *A Place for Strangers: Towards a History of Australian Aboriginal Being*, Cambridge University Press, 1993.

Australian Aboriginal anthropology has fared better than anthropology in other countries in that there have been a number of women observers of Aboriginal societies – Nancy Munn, Jane Goodale, Phyllis Kaberry, Catherine Berndt, Ursula McConnell, Annette Hamilton and others.) Diane Bell has, to some extent, redressed the balance in her admirable book *Daughters of the Dreaming*,[37] but much more remains to be done.

As is so often the case in Australian Aboriginal culture, mutuality and complementarity and interdependence are central. One cannot, for example, understand 'ownership' of the land without taking into account the complementary roles of what some groups call *kirda* and *kurtungulu* – so-called 'owners' and 'managers' – and one cannot really understand Aboriginal religions without seeing how both men's 'business' and women's 'business' complement each other. As Noel Wallace has noted of the Pitjantjatjara people:

> There are practically no man-only ceremonies that may commence without women being there. They are not only present, but certain women of knowledge and seniority are involved in the commencement of ceremony. Then, at the correct time, all the women leave and at some distant place commence a complementary women-only ceremony. Later, all come together for a common conclusion.[38]

Wallace also makes the more general point that, while the aim of men's ceremonies is to bring them into communication with the Ancestor Spirits 'to perpetuate the harmony between human beings and country', the aim of women's ceremonies is to 'ensure the continuation of their race' through communication with the Ancestor Spirits.[39] Just as, then, we cannot understand human sexuality without appreciating the complementarity of female and male sexuality, so also with female and male Aboriginal religion and spirituality. However, as we have noted, a major difficulty here, which arises directly out of a fundamental cultural difference between the western anthropological observer and the Australian Aboriginal observed, is that within Aboriginal society women's religion is kept secret from men, and vice versa. The attempt, then,

---

[37] Diane Bell, *Daughters of the Dreaming*, Melbourne, McPhee Gribble, 1983.
[38] Max Charlesworth, Richard Kimber and Noel Wallace, *Ancestor Spirits: Aspects of Australian Aboriginal Life and Spirituality*, Geelong, Deakin University Press, 1990, p. 65.
[39] Ibid. p. 64.

by a western anthropologist to describe fully, in an even-handed way, both women's and men's religious business, violates the Australian Aborigines' religiously based code of secrecy which forbids that mutual disclosure.

THE DRAMATIC AND EXOTIC

It has been a general feature of the anthropological approach that it has tended to focus on the most dramatic and exotic aspects of other cultures and religions, since it was thought that they provided a key to the whole cultural system and the whole religious world which it was practically impossible to study in a comprehensive way. As Clifford, speaking of the 'new ethnography' of the 1930s and 1940s, notes:

Since culture, seen as a complex whole was too much to master in a short research span, the new ethnographer intended to focus thematically on particular institutions. The aim was not to contribute to a complete inventory or description of custom but rather to get at the whole through one or more of its parts.[40]

Inevitably this meant that the more dramatic aspects of religion – Clifford instances the Kula ring or the Naven ceremony – were singled out for attention.

This approach has had a distorting effect upon our view of Australian Aboriginal religions, in that the commonplace and humdrum and domestic aspects of Aboriginal spiritual life have been de-emphasised, while what one might call the Ottonian aspects (after Rudolf Otto's famous definition of religion as the sphere of the 'numinous' which is itself defined as 'mysterium tremendum et fascinans') have been correspondingly exaggerated. Although there is a strong sense of the 'numinous' in Aboriginal religion, and some real fear and awe about spirits and spiritually dangerous places, it is also characterised by a sense of ease and familiarity between humans and the sacred realm. Apparently domestic (non-dramatic and non-exotic) events and practices such as sand drawing and sculpture, body painting, children's games,

---

[40] *The Predicament of Culture*, p. 31.

butchering animals and apportioning parts of animals for eating, cooking methods etc., are often pregnant with religious meaning.

SECRECY

I have alluded to the difficulty for the western anthropologist of disclosing information about Aboriginal women's religion to men, and vice versa. For western anthropologists, observing the canons of scientific rationalism, there can be no secrets, since anthropology is committed to total public disclosure of information about its 'subjects'. But, for the Australian Aborigines there are secrets not only between men and women, but also between old and young, the initiated and the non-initiated, insiders and outsiders. Those secrets can be divulged only to people in the appropriate situation, and severe penalties are inflicted on those who break secrecy. Speaking of the Yolngu people of north-east Arnhem Land, Howard Morphy shows how pervasive secrecy is and how it is basically a religious phenomenon in that it is necessary to cope with and control dangerous religious knowledge. 'Secrecy in Yolngu society', Morphy says,

is clearly related to political power and authority. But even if control of religious knowledge enhances or provides a basis for male control of other aspects of society, its value cannot be reduced to this. The Yolngu view would be more that certain things are secret because they are powerful rather than the other way around. The men control the ceremonial ground because it is closest to ancestral power: they know how to manipulate that power through their ownership and control of the songs, dances, paintings and ceremonies. The powers are dangerous for them but more dangerous for others, who require the mediation of the men. However, the men's own power stems from and is supported by their control of the ceremonies and their closeness to the *wanggarr* ancestors.[41]

The paradoxical situation of the western anthropologist, attempting to investigate a culture and religious system pervaded by religious-based secrecy, is to some extent paralleled by the situation

---

[41] Howard Morphy, *Ancestral Connections: Art and an Aboriginal System of Knowledge*, University of Chicago Press, 1991, pp. 95–6. See also Ian Keen, *Knowledge and Secrecy in an Aboriginal Religion*, Clarendon Press, Oxford, 1994.

in contemporary Aboriginal art, where traditional motifs and designs with secret-sacred significance are used both in Aboriginal contexts and in the context of paintings made for the white commercial market. In many cases, paintings may have exactly the same form and design, but the one used in an Aboriginal funeral rite will have a completely different meaning for the Aboriginal participants from that of the painting produced for commercial sale in the white art market and bought by an art connoisseur in New York.[42]

To return to the idea of secrecy: as we have seen, the western cultural belief that scientific information about people and cultures and religious systems is public and that everything should be divulged, runs up against the Aboriginal cultural belief that a religiously based code of secrecy forbids complete disclosure of many crucial aspects of Australian Aboriginal life and religion. Even if the anthropologist has an obligation to respect Aboriginal sensitivities about secret and sacred matters, he or she has, *qua* anthropologist, to make it seem that something approaching the western cultural ideal of full public disclosure is possible. The western anthropologist cannot rest content, as an Aborigine must, with reporting that certain important aspects of Aboriginal life are secret and cannot be discussed openly or publicly. From this point of view the very attempt to investigate Aboriginal culture and Aboriginal religion necessarily puts a 'public' construction upon something that is essentially non-public and secretive. In practice, of course, compromises and accommodations are possible and a white observer may be given permission by an Aboriginal group to make public a good deal of information. But there are limits (increasingly severe) as to what may be divulged, and the paradox I have just described remains.

THE UNITY OF AUSTRALIAN ABORIGINAL CULTURE
AND RELIGION

An assumption that has been widespread among observers of Australian Aboriginal culture and religion is that culture and

---

[42] Howard Morphy, *Ancestral Connections*, ch. 2, 'Art for Sale'.

religion were more or less uniform across pre-colonial Australia. It was acknowledged that there might be local and regional variants, but it was supposed that there were central universal themes that were common to all and that defined them as being 'Aboriginal'. But, as Keen notes:

> it should not be assumed that there were attributes or essential features common to all regions. Social life across the Aboriginal population may never have formed an integrated system across the continent.

All the recent evidence goes to show that regional social forms were extremely varied and that there was a dynamic interaction between them.[43] There is, no doubt, a general resemblance between the various regional cultures and religions, just as there is a general resemblance between the distinct languages that make up the linguistic group called 'Australian'. But, as noted above, it would be more accurate to speak of Aboriginal Australian *cultures* in the plural and Aboriginal *religions* in the plural.

Some of the aspects of anthropological methodology discussed above have, of course, influenced and shaped the study of other cultures generally, and are not peculiar to the study of Australian Aboriginal cultures and religions. However, the latter has been affected in an especially profound way because, almost from the beginnings of anthropology as a discipline, Australian Aboriginal religions were recognised as being among the oldest forms of religious belief and practice and as a kind of 'test case'. Then again, as we have seen, ethnographic evidence about the Australian Aborigines came on stream just at the crucial time to meet the demands of Frazerian and Durkheimian theory. As a result, if all primitive cultures and religions have, to some extent, been 'constructed' by western anthropologists, Australian Aboriginal culture and religion has been more constructed than others!

---

[43] Ian Keen, 'Ubiquitous Ubiety of Dubious Uniformity', *The Australian Journal of Anthropology*, 4:2, 1993, 106–7. In his most recent work, *Knowledge and Secrecy in an Aboriginal Religion*, Keen has pointed to tendencies among certain contemporary Aboriginal groups to adopt more inclusive attitudes in the religious realm. See p. 256: 'Yolngu have recently begun to favour universalistic religious forms, which united groups and moieties, attempted to overcome the separation of men and women through religious secrecy, and which linked Yolngu to Balanda (white people).' One of the Yolngu groups has in fact identified its most sacred symbol – the 'tree/wood' (dharpa) – and the Christian Cross.

THE INVENTION OF THE 'DREAMING'

By way of conclusion, I would like to sketch out how this anthropological construction has been responsible for shaping what is, to western observers, the key concept of Australian Aboriginal religion, the so-called 'Dreaming' or 'Dreamtime'. The term itself is an invention, in that it does not directly translate any of the Aboriginal terms for the complex set of phenomena in question. In other words, the Aboriginal equivalents for dreaming while asleep are not applied by Australian Aborigines to the fundamental religious phenomena. Baldwin Spencer seems to have been the first to have used the term 'the Dream Time' to translate the Aranda-speaking people's term *alcheringa* or *altjiranga*. This term was employed by the Aranda people to describe the primordial time when the Ancestor Spirits 'at the beginning of things' shaped the physical world and at the same time laid down the ethical, social, religious, ceremonial and ritual 'Law', or way of life, to be followed by Aboriginal groups. (Since the way of life laid down by the Ancestor Spirits differed from group to group, we should speak, perhaps, of 'Laws' instead of the 'Law'.) Thus, the Aranda phrase *altjiranga ngambakala* has the connotation of 'having originated out of one's own eternity', 'immortal', 'uncreated'. Baldwin Spencer seems to have been confused because a similar Aranda phrase *altjira rama* means 'to see eternal things', or 'to see or dream eternal things'. Thus the idea of seeing eternal things in dreams was transferred to the primordial time and the primordial actors, so that the former came to be called 'the Dreamtime' or 'Dreaming' and the actors (the Ancestor Spirits) came to be called 'Dreamings' and their mythic journeyings 'Dreaming Tracks'.

However, if the concept of 'the Dreaming' originated in a confusion, it was soon adopted enthusiastically by other anthropologists and became embedded in anthropological and popular discourse. (In fact, many Australian Aborigines themselves now use the term.) It is probably too late to get rid of the term 'the Dreaming', but it remains true that it distorts our understanding of the complex set of phenomena it purports to refer to. First, it makes it seem as though what is referred to is a unitary phenomenon; second, it suggests that the realities it refers to belong to what

Lévy-Bruhl called the realm of the 'pre-logical', the fantastic domain where the laws of logic do not apply; third, it suggests that those realities are mythical in the pejorative 'once upon a time' sense and that we are dealing with something that is fictive or unreal; fourth, in so far as the term refers to a primordial period it gives it a prehistoric sense as though the events of the 'Dreamtime' occurred a long time ago; fifth, it also suggests that what happened in the primordial period strictly determines what happens in the present so that 'the Dreaming' is an essentially conservative principle. (Quite apart from this, there has been a vulgarisation of the concept of 'the Dreaming' in various 'New Age' interpretations. Thus 'the Dreaming' has been seen as related to the Jungian theory of archetypes, the Hindu idea of *karma*, 'Green' theories about humans and nature, neo-Christian ideas about 'creation spirituality' and so on.)

In actual fact, the reality to which the misleading term 'the Dreaming' refers comprises a complex set of phenomena; it includes the primordial creative shaping of the world by the Ancestor Spirits, though this is not seen by Australian Aborigines in a prehistoric sense; it also includes the giving of a 'Law' or way of life to particular groups and of a personal way or 'Law' that derives from the circumstances of an individual's 'spirit conception'. Again, far from being 'pre-logical' or unreal or dream-like, what is referred to by the term 'Dreaming' is for Aborigines the most intensely real thing there is. Further, it is eternally present and immanent. Elkin has put the matter very well: the Dreaming, he says, is not just 'a long-past period in a time series when the landscape took its present form and when life filled the void. It is rather the ever-present, unseen, ground of being, of existence.' And he goes on to say:

The concept is not of a 'horizontal' line extending back chronologically through a series of pasts, but rather of a 'vertical' line in which the past underlies and is within the present. As the top of an iceberg is seen and is powerful because of its great unseen mass moving beneath the surface, so man and nature are sustained by the ever-present, latent power of the Dreaming. An Aboriginal man expresses this belief in his ritual, mythology and symbolism, through which the Dreaming becomes sacramentally visible and potent.[44]

---

[44] 'Elements of Australian Philosophy', p. 93.

VITALISM IN AUSTRALIAN ABORIGINAL RELIGION

Although Elkin nicely captures the immanent character of 'the Dreaming', one could use more vitalistic terms to define it as an eternal and uncreated and immanent spiritual power or *life-force* which manifests itself first in the Ancestor Spirits and uses them as its vehicle at a certain phase in the creative process, and then resides in the land and in living creatures as a source of all fertility and fecundity.

From an ethical perspective, in a recent essay on the Yarralin people, the anthropologist Deborah Bird Rose claims that the concept of the Dreaming implies that: '(a) all parts of the cosmos (animals, humans, sun etc.) are alive; (b) all parts are conscious, that is are capable of knowing and acting; and (c) all parts are related to other parts, either directly or indirectly'. From this Rose derives four principles which 'form the basis to Yarralin people's concept of morality. These are the principles of balance, symmetry, autonomy and response.' These principles, she claims, relate to an ultimate belief about the meaning of life which the Yarralin people see as 'the nurturance of all life'. The principle of balance, she goes on:

indicates that no part shall overcome other parts, but rather all parts shall act upon each other in such a way as to contain, but not destroy each other. The related principle of symmetry indicates that when and if parts of the system oppose each other in a hostile or potentially destructive manner, boundaries must be drawn in such a way that the parts are equal or symmetrical. Autonomy, as a moral principle, indicates that no part of the system is subservient to, or dominated by, any other part. The principle of response prevents autonomy from becoming chaotic by indicating that each part of the system must pay attention, and respond to other parts.[45]

Again, David Turner, discussing the Groote Eylandt people's concept of *amawurena*, has this to say:

The essential point is this: the land is imbued with Eternity; so are People and Natural Species. *Amawurena* impregnates them all. *Amawurena* is something you can't touch, you can't see, you can't feel, but it's there . . . It can take the shape of country, of natural species, of *numeraga*. It assumes

---

[45] Deborah Bird Rose, 'The Saga of Captain Cook: Morality in Aboriginal and European Law', *Australian Aboriginal Studies*, 2, 1984, 30.

different forms in different countries, in different species, in different *numeraga*. It is transmitted through a kinship line – father to children – sanctified by marriage. A differentiated part of it is in each of us in both an individual and collective sense. Everyone in his or her own collectivity has a differentiated part of it as does the collectivity as such. This is what makes us all 'like' each other, that is 'alike in our differences'. In its differentiated form, *amawurena* is what we worship.[46]

Australian Aboriginal religion is profoundly immanentist in that the primordial spiritual power is *in* the cosmos – in the land, in animate creatures and in human beings. There are no transcendent gods: the Ancestor Spirits are not gods but rather vehicles of the primordial spiritual power and they are not moral exemplars (like Buddha or Jesus). It is the land or territory of each group, shaped by the Ancestor Spirits and impregnated by them with spiritual power, that is the mediator of that power which is necessary for the continuance and flourishing of all life. Tony Swain has wittily described the Aboriginal religious outlook as 'geosophical'; in other words it is based upon the conviction that 'all wisdom and truth is fixed in the earth'. Speaking of the Central Australian people, the Warlpiri, Swain remarks:

Despite the fact Warlpiri do not trace an unbroken lineage back to their supernatural progenitors, they nonetheless have an immediate kinship with them which is *mediated by the potency of the land itself.* It thus follows that Warlpiri religious identity is more a question of geography than theology.[47]

It is worthwhile remarking that Aboriginal languages are also linked with the land. Thus the Jawoyn language is associated with a tract of land and if a person is associated with a place in that land, he or she is thereby associated with the language. As it has been put: 'Jawoyn people are Jawoyn not because they speak Jawoyn, but because they are linked to places to which the Jawoyn language is linked.'[48]

---

[46] David Turner, 'The Incarnation of Nambirrima', in Tony Swain and Deborah Bird Rose eds., *Aboriginal Australians and Christian Missions: Ethnographic and Historical Studies*, Adelaide, The Australian Association for the Study of Religions, 1988, p. 475.

[47] Tony Swain, 'The Ghost of Space: Reflections on Warlpiri Christian Iconography and Ritual', in Tony Swain and Deborah Bird Rose eds. *Aboriginal Australians and Christian Missions*, pp. 459–60.

[48] Alan Rumsey, 'Language and Territoriality in Aboriginal Australia', in Michael Walsh and Colin Yallop eds., *Language and Culture in Aboriginal Australia*, Canberra, Aboriginal Studies Press, 1993, p. 200.

As remarked before, the anthropologically invented term 'the Dreaming' obscures the rich complexity of the fundamental metaphysical and ethical realities to which it refers. If it were possible, it would be better if we got rid of the term altogether and recognised that complexity.

CONCLUSION

The picture presented here of the anthropological construction or invention of Australian Aboriginal religion may seem to be a negative and sceptical one in that it emphasises how much our past view of Australian Aboriginal religion has been distorted by the methodologically based misapprehensions of anthropologists. There have, of course, been anthropological approaches which have provided alternative views to those we have been discussing here. The work of the remarkable anthropologist, T. G. H. Strehlow, from the 1930s to the 1960s, is worthy of notice here. Strehlow was the son of a German Lutheran missionary and scholar, Pastor Carl Strehlow, who worked among the Aranda peoples in central Australia and wrote studies of Aboriginal myths and songs (all the while steadfastly refusing to be present at Aranda ceremonies) and the Aranda language. T. G. H. Strehlow was brought up among the Aranda and always identified very strongly with them (he belonged, he claimed, to the important totem group of the Twins of Ntarea and was a 'true Aranda'). Even when he became Professor of Anthropology at the University of Adelaide in South Australia, his main interest was in sketching out the conditions of possibility of a Christian/Western and Aranda ecumenism, and what a recent observer has called 'an environ-mentally-attuned post-colonial poetics'.[49] In his great work *Songs of Central Australia*,[50] published in 1971, Strehlow provided an account of Aranda ceremonial songs and linked them, rather fancifully, to the Homeric myths and the Germanic myths of northern Europe. As Carter has said:

Triangulating between a colonialist heritage, a migrant present and the desirability of a bicultural future, Strehlow attempted to create a mode of

---

[49] Paul Carter, *The Lie of the Land*, p. 71. Carter's sensitive study of Strehlow's project is perhaps the best account of this whole doomed enterprise.   [50] Sydney, 1971.

memorialisation more adequate to the representation of his, and his adopted society's colonial condition. Affiliating himself to Aranda traditions, he did not forget his own learned Western traditions, but made the meeting place of the two his life's work.[51]

Apart from Strehlow's work, Fr. E. A. Worms, R. M. and C. H. Berndt have, for example, given us other, less restricted, views of Aboriginal religion. Above all, the remarkable writings of W. E. H. Stanner have shown how serious and sophisticated a system Australian Aboriginal religion really is.[52] Again, as mentioned above, contemporary anthropologists such as Diane Bell, Eric Kolig, Deborah Bird Rose, David Turner and others have shown the uniquely different character of Aboriginal religion. It would be hard to imagine, for example, a religious system that is further removed from Judaeo-Christianity. In general the religions of the Australian Aborigines remind us that the religions of peoples in relatively small and simple societies can be just as complex and sophisticated as the so-called world-religions – Hinduism, Buddhism, Judaism, Christianity, Islam and so on – and just as worthy of serious study and ecumenical exchange.[53]

Further, Tony Swain has recently written what is really the first systematic philosophical study of Australian Aboriginal religion: *A Place for Strangers: Towards a History of Australian Aboriginal Being.*[54] As has been noted, Swain's thesis is that for the Warlpiri people the cosmic and social orders have no temporal or historical dimension but are centred on space and place and 'country'.

Nevertheless, despite these notable exceptions, it remains largely true that the anthropological perspectives I have been mainly concerned with here, have had a dominant effect in shaping both scholarly and popular views of the Aboriginal religious system. Indeed, in various subtle ways they continue to shape those views.

However, if we can now discern how much our views of Australian Aboriginal religions have been invented or constructed,

[51] *The Lie of the Land*, p. 26.
[52] On Stanner and the other observers mentioned see Max Charlesworth, Introduction to *Religion in Aboriginal Australia*, St Lucia, University of Queensland Press, 1984.
[53] As an example of ecumenical, Christian–Australian Aboriginal dialogue see Eugene Stockton, *The Aboriginal Gift: Spirituality for a Nation*, Sydney, E. J. Dwyer, 1995.
[54] Cambridge University Press, 1993. See the critical review of Swain's book by Ian Keen in *The Australian Journal of Anthropology*, 4:2, 1993, 96–110.

we should not think that *we* are in some kind of privileged position that enables us to understand Aboriginal culture and religions 'in their own terms' or 'as they really are'. In fact, we also are inescapably involved in the business of inter-cultural negotiation and translation and we cannot really avoid the fact that *our* views of Australian Aboriginal culture and religion are also constructed or invented in various ways. We smile now at the *naïveté* of the early English painters who painted the Australian landscape as though it were like the Lake District or the Scottish Highlands; but we do not notice the cultural filters and lenses we use in our own paintings.

To recognise this fact does not, however, lead to any kind of cultural relativism which would mean that people were locked up in their own cultural worlds and prevented from any kind of mutual understanding or interchange with other cultures. What it means is that any inter-cultural understanding (especially where religion and spirituality are involved) is, while possible, very difficult. A comparison with linguistic translation may be helpful here. It is always possible in principle to understand another language in a general way and to translate it into the terms of one's own language. We are not enclosed or imprisoned in our respective languages so that no kind of translation is possible. (In fact, the notion of total untranslatablity is absurd, for how could we *know* that a language was totally untranslatable?) However, it is very difficult to translate certain forms of language, for example, poetry, into another language. The best we can do is to provide analogies – using, for example, the poetic forms and styles and devices peculiar to our language – to give an idea (often very oblique and remote) of what is being expressed, through very different poetic forms and conventions, in another language. So also with translating Australian Aboriginal religious concepts into western European terms. Once again, the best we can do is to provide analogies (for example, the land or country plays the same role, mediating spiritual power, in Aboriginal religion as Jesus Christ, mediating grace, plays in Christianity). Some analogies will be more illuminating and fruitful than others, but none will be able to claim to be the 'true' picture or to convey the total meaning of the original.

From another point of view, we proceed by a kind of *via negativa*, that is we come to know what Australian religions are like by knowing how utterly unlike they are to any of our western European ideas about religion or to the great 'world religions' of Asia and the Middle East. From this point of view, well-meaning syncretistic attempts to mix Aboriginal religious concepts with superficially similar Christian or other religious concepts, are not really helpful. That is why a discerning comparative religion perspective (conspicuously absent so far) is so important in the study of Australian Aboriginal religion.

While being duly (though critically) grateful to our anthropologists then, what is needed in the future is a more philosophical and comparativist approach to Australian Aboriginal religion which will enable us look at issues in Aboriginal religions which have, so to speak, been screened out by the approach and methods of past social anthropology. Anthropologists have, quite legitimately, their own methodological focusses, but they necessarily leave out of account issues of a philosophical–theological kind: for example, the conditions of possibility of the realm of 'the divine', the foundation of the ethical order, the existence of evil (both physical and moral), moral conflict and tragedy, personal autonomy in religion and enlightenment or 'salvation', freedom and fatalism, space and time and history in religious cosmology, the concept of truth in religion. Stanner once remarked that for the Australian Aborigines 'life is a joyous thing with maggots at the centre',[55] and it is understanding the meaning of philosophical–theological intuitions like this that requires an approach that goes beyond social anthropology.

[55] Cited in L. R. Hiatt ed., *Australian Aboriginal Mythology*, Canberra, Australian Institute of Aboriginal Studies, p. 11.

Universal and local elements in religion

INTRODUCTION

Kierkegaard says somewhere that Hegel built a gigantic edifice of theory and then lived in a little hole alongside it. Kierkegaard's *ad hominem* sarcasm was intended to show that Hegel's philosophy had no relevance for the business of living; but, in a certain sense, one could say that it is strictly impossible to live in any house of theory: the abstract air is too thin to breathe. One cannot live in a world of universality, where universal principles are supposed to apply to all beings (including human beings) at all times and places, any more than one can speak a universal language. In the last resort, one has to *live* in a particular place and culture and one has to speak a local language.

As Aristotle keeps reminding us throughout the *Nicomachean Ethics*, ethics is a practical body of knowledge, for ultimately a decision about good and bad ways of human living has to be made in particular circumstances here and now. General rules, about temperance and justice and courage are, of course, necessary, but I, this moral agent, have then to judge what temperance and justice and courage mean in the specific situation in which I find myself. That judgment requires imaginative interpretation: for example, is returning a weapon to a friend, who has since become psychotic and suicidal, properly described as a matter of 'justice' or rather as an irresponsible breach of true friendship?

The same is true in the religious sphere, for religious truths (which are implicitly or explicitly universal) have to be lived out in local contexts or traditions. In so far as they make claims to be *true*, religious belief systems have universal import and transcend local situations both in space and time; but they are lived or practised in local situations. Even (one might say, especially) the so-called 'world religions' with their explicitly universalistic claims or pretensions, are put into practice in local communities or traditions and are adapted and interpreted in the light of local needs and exigencies and experience. The history of early Christianity with its small church communities – at Corinth, Ephesus, Rome, Jerusalem, Antioch etc. – all with their own very different traditions, is typical in this regard. The Christian community at Corinth that St Paul wrote to was vastly different from the community he addressed at Ephesus. Again, as we know, the texts that make up the Synoptic Gospels, which subsequently came to have universal significance in the Church, were profoundly influenced by the local situations in which they were written. The preaching and life and death of Jesus had to be received and interpreted by believers in those situations and endowed with a special status. That is, of course, why scripture exegetes have focussed on those local circumstances in order to understand the full meaning of the texts.[1]

Later, from the second century onwards, there was an immense effort within Christianity to ensure that the various local traditions were in broad doctrinal agreement. The 'creeds', the church Councils and the development of central ecclesiastical power by the Bishop of Rome and the Roman bureaucracy, were all attempts to formulate criteria for 'orthodoxy'. The marks of the 'true Church' were that it was 'one, holy, catholic and apostolic' and intense efforts were made to ensure the unity and catholicity (or universality) of the Christian churches. However, the local traditions persisted and large and significant differences emerged between the Latin and eastern churches and then within those two great blocs of Christendom. Even though the local Christian churches or communities acknowledged the same credal formulations emanating from the central authorities in Rome or Constantinople, they often interpreted them in practice in very different ways.

---

[1] See Henry Chadwick, *The Early Church*, Harmondsworth, Penguin Books, revised edition, 1993. See also Lisa Sowle Cahill, 'The New Testament and Ethics: Communities of Social Change', *Interpretation*, 44, 1990, 383–95.

The dialectical tension in Christianity between the universalising and the localising tendencies was, of course, exacerbated by the Reformation and its aftermath. In broad terms one could say that in the Reformed churches the local triumphed over the universal, while in the Roman Catholic Church (after the Counter Reformation) the universal prevailed over the local. In the latter church there was in the nineteenth century a systematic attempt to prevent local traditions from emerging through a determined strengthening of papal power and control (for example, through the declaration of the doctrine of papal infallibility at the First Vatican Council, and the expansion of papal teaching authority or the 'magisterium'). One could interpret the work of the Second Vatican Council as an attempt to give back to bishops and local church structures and communities (the 'people of God') some of the power they had lost. Since the Council there has been a concerted attempt to restore central control in the name of 'unity' and 'catholicity', although there have also been strong localising tendencies within the Roman Catholic Church, such as the development of 'liberation theology', the idea of 'basic Christian communities', the thesis that the message and values of the Gospels must be 'inculturated', that is, expressed in terms of the particular cultural setting in which they are received, and the partial recognition that tolerance of creative (and 'loyal') dissent within the church is essential.

I have been speaking so far of the universalising and localising tendencies within religions in terms of one kind of religion, Christianity, and one species of Christianity, Roman Catholicism. But, while the tension between the two tendencies has been especially marked in the history of Christianity, and above all in the Roman Catholic Church, it has also been present in other religions such as Hinduism, Buddhism, Judaism and Islam. One can, in fact, say, as was remarked before, that in all religions, including so-called primal religions like those of the Australian Aborigines, there is a universal element just from the fact that a religion makes truth claims, and there is a local element just from the fact that a religion is received and interpreted and lived out experientially in a specific context or situation or tradition. Religion, like ethics, is (to use Aristotle's term) a 'practical' business where general or universal considerations are brought to bear upon concrete and particular matters, and this requires a judgment based upon imaginative interpretation ('this is what God's revelation, or the Buddha's teaching, or the Taoist "Way" means in these circumstances in which our community lives'). In ethics we need both general rules or principles about justice and temperance and the other virtues, and also what Aristotle calls 'practical wisdom' (*phronesis*), that is the ability to judge that this is what justice or temperance means in these circumstances. In religion also we need the universal element, the doctrinal truths that are central to any revelation and that ensure some kind of continuity between the various expressions of that revelation, and the local element, the traditions that enshrine the ways in which people receive and interpret and develop and live out that revelation in the particular circumstances in which they find themselves.

Keeping the universal and local elements in proper balance is difficult. If the universalising tendency in a religion becomes too dominant, then the identity and continuity (and 'purity') of the religion may be preserved, but at a fearful cost. Centralisation and the emasculation of local initiatives, institutional pharisaism and legalism and distrust of the Spirit, suppression of dissent, fear of any change, uniformity instead of authentic unity, are some of the consequences. On the other hand, if the local element becomes dominant, local interpretations of the central religious revelation may become so idiosyncratic that their connection with the central revelation and the mainstream interpretations may be lost. Sectarianism is the result and that is just as destructive to true religion as the consequences of universalism.

Seventeenth- and eighteenth-century sectarianism in England provides a vivid picture of the dangers of localism with the proliferation of small and eccentric religious bodies. For example, in a recent book on the religious background of William Blake's thought, the English historian E. P. Thompson (citing a contemporary document) provides the following directory to some of the seventeenth- and eighteenth-century English sects:

Quakers, Muggletonians, Millennaries, Sabbatarians or Seventh-Day Men, Thraskites, Adamists (whose meeting place was 'Paradise' and whose devotions were made in nakedness), Seekers, Ranters (who condemned the Bible), Brownists, Tryonists (vegetarians), the 'Church of the First Born' (Behemists), Salmonists, 'Heavenly Father Men' (whose whole emphasis was on Mercy) and 'Children of the New-Birth', much given to meditation and to 'Visions of Angels and Representations'. And others. The 'Sweet Singers of Israel were "very poetically given, turning all into Rhime, and singing all their Worship, They meet in an Ale-House and eat, drink and smoak"'. There was also a 'Family of Love' who believed that the soul was an 'Emanation of the Deity' which (at death) is lost in the 'Eternal Ocean of Beings'.[2]

This picture of eighteenth-century English sectarianism could, of course, be more than matched by contemporary, Californian and other, forms. And, once again, sectarianism is not something peculiar to Christianity.

The universalists point, of course, to the wild excesses of the sectarians, both ancient and modern, as a compelling reason for maintaining 'orthodoxy': if the central religious authority's interest in orthodoxy is relaxed, so they argue, even in the smallest way, then the vices of sectarianism will follow inevitably. The localists, on the other hand, point to the consequences of universalism mentioned before – institutional pharisaism, the suffocation of creative dissent, uniformity instead of authentic unity etc. Both sides maintain themselves and justify their positions by focussing on the excesses of the other.

FOUNDATIONALISM AND ANTI-FOUNDATIONALISM

An analogous form of this debate has recently been played out in the philosophical arena with the critical questioning of the universalistic values of the European 'enlightenment', and more particularly in discussions about the foundations of knowledge. With regard to the latter, what might be called the Cartesian project – the attempt to provide an indubitable, self-justifying, foundation for human knowledge – has been subjected to attacks from various quarters, and an attempt has been made to erect 'local knowledge' as the only real basis we have for the various forms of human knowledge.

[2] E. P. Thompson, *Witness Against the Beast: William Blake and the Moral Law*, Cambridge University Press, 1993, p. 55.

This anti-foundationalist and anti-universalistic critique has been developed within very different perspectives: for example, Wittgenstein's later philosophy with its central idea of 'forms of life' as the contextual determinant of meaning; Saussurean linguistics and the various forms of semiological theory, associated with Claude Lévi-Strauss and Roland Barthes, which see language as the primary model for knowledge; Michel Foucault's concept of the socially constructed thought and power structures which he calls 'epistemes' and which determine what is to count as 'truth' in any area of discourse; Thomas Kuhn's thesis that scientific knowledge is governed by 'paradigms' tacitly sanctioned by the scientific community in particular epochs so that development in science is not evolutionary or cumulative but, due to the sudden and unpredictable shifts in paradigms, 'revolutionary'; Rorty's radical conventionalism and pragmatism; Derrida's deconstruction project (perhaps the most dramatic and far-reaching form of anti-foundationalism); the sociology of science movement (if, indeed, it can be called a 'movement') associated with Bruno Latour, Karen Knorr-Cetina and others, and which sees scientific knowledge as being socio-culturally 'constructed'; the anti-foundationalist tendency in contemporary literary theory (Stanley Fish and others); the anti-positivist 'interpretivist' tendency of Ronald Dworkin and others in contemporary jurisprudence.

I do not think that it is helpful to see these various tendencies as part of a general coherent 'movement'. However, there are affinities between them. To take some examples at random: the American philosopher of science, Hilary Putnam, argues that without public norms shared by a group and constituting a 'form of life', language and even thought itself would be impossible. Similarly, within science

judgment that special relativity and quantum electro-dynamics are the most successful physical theories we have is one which is made by authorities whom the society has appointed and whose authority is recognised by a host of practices and ceremonies, and in that sense institutionalised.[3]

---

[3] In A. F. Heath ed., *Scientific Explanation*, Oxford University Press, 1981, p. 101.

Again, with regard to the foundations of ethics, Bernard Williams, criticising Kant's foundationalist and universalistic view of morality, notes that

> Hegel admirably criticised the 'abstract' Kantian morality and contrasted it with the notion of *Sittlichkeit,* a concretely determined ethical existence that was expressed in the local folkways, a form of life that made particular sense to the people living in it. The conception inevitably raises the question of how local those folkways can properly remain, and whether they cannot be criticised, ranked, or transcended. But the Hegelian problem is the right problem at least to this extent: it asks how a concretely experienced form of life can be extended, rather than considering how a universal program is to be applied.[4]

Further, the anthropologist Clifford Geertz has argued that the 'local knowledge' which we recognise in so-called primitive societies as being culturally grounded, can be extended to the belief systems of the anthropological observers themselves. In other words, anthropology itself is a form of culturally grounded local knowledge.[5] Prima facie, this makes any transcultural knowledge, of the kind claimed by traditional anthropology and other social sciences, difficult to justify, though Geertz resists the idea that this necessarily leads to any kind of pernicious relativism.

Finally, the American literary theorist, Stanley Fish, argues that in literary interpretation there is no 'higher law or overarching theory' to which we can appeal for justification and which will act as a foundation. As he puts it:

> anti-foundationalism teaches that questions of fact, truth, correctness, validity and clarity can neither be posed nor answered in reference to some extracontextual, ahistorical, nonsituational reality, or rule, or law, or value; rather, anti-foundationalism asserts, all of these matters are intelligible and debatable only within the precincts of the contexts or situations or paradigms or communities that give them their local and changeable shape.[6]

---

[4] Bernard Williams, *Ethics and the Limits of Philosophy*, Cambridge, Mass., Harvard University Press, 1985, p. 104.

[5] Clifford Geertz, *Local Knowledge: Further Essays in Interpretive Anthropology*, New York, Basic Books, 1983.

[6] Stanley Fish, *Doing What Comes Naturally*, Durham, N. C., Duke University Press, 1989, p. 345.

There are grave problems about the idea that the quest for any kind of extra-contextual or universal foundation for knowledge in general, or scientific knowledge in particular, or for ethical or aesthetic values, or for legal interpretation, is illusory and a wild-goose chase. There are also problems about the complementary thesis that local (non-universal) knowledge in these various domains provides the only 'foundation' that is possible. The main difficulty that confronts anti-foundationalism in all its forms is to show how it escapes relativism or epistemological sectarianism. For example, if Fish is right, then at first sight it would seem that the aesthetic value of any piece of literature is what an 'interpretive community' deems it to be. There are other related difficulties, for example, how is it possible to stand in judgment on a form of local knowledge and judge it as debased or corrupt or deviant? Or do we have to accept everything in local knowledge just as it is? Do we, for example, have to accept the ethical folkways, to use Hegel's term, just as they are? Derrida, we may remember, argues that the western philosophical tradition has been systematically distorted by 'logocentrism', but how is he able to judge that this is a distortion unless he allows a critical function to human reason which enables it to transcend its local context? How can we, from *within* the western philosophical tradition, stand in judgment *on* that tradition unless we are able to transcend the domain of local knowledge? If we cannot find a place for critical and transcendent reason must we, as just remarked, accept everything in the various forms of local knowledge; and, if we say that, do we not thereby sanctify the *status quo* and make any change in local knowledge unintelligible? As many critics have pointed out, Thomas Kuhn, one of the protagonists of local knowledge in the scientific domain, finds it difficult to explain why and how scientific paradigms, by reference to which the practice of science in any one epoch is 'justified', undergo 'revolutionary' change.

THE SPECTRE OF RELATIVISM

Is the appeal to local knowledge then necessarily flawed by relativism, and is the only way of escape from relativism and situational particularity some kind of appeal to universal or supra-local foundations or norms in the light of which we can judge and criticise local knowledge?

To get to grips with these questions it is helpful to look at Aristotle's approach to ethics in the *Nicomachean Ethics*.[7] There Aristotle warns us that we must not expect ethics to have any kind of strictly necessary and universal basis, so that any attempt to provide, in the manner of Kant, a metaphysical ground for ethics is out of the question. Instead, Aristotle presents us with a picture of a person with certain central moral and intellectual 'excellences' or virtues. These are the excellences that we recognise that any human person should have since they show human beings at their most 'fine and noble'. Aristotle does not claim that these excellences are derivable from an analysis of 'human nature' viewed as some kind of fixed essence, and equally he does not say that they are simply the qualities of character recognised by the Athenian society of his time. Rather, he suggests that there are certain general or transcultural human needs and interests that have to be taken into account when we are are reflecting on what is good for human beings and on what makes them flourish as human beings. Different cultures and different societies may perform that task of reflection in different ways and reach very different solutions, but those various local solutions will not be (as the relativist wants to claim) incommensurable or incomparable. In other words, it will be possible to compare the various interpretive responses and to stand in critical judgment on them precisely because they are interpretive responses to a common set of general human interests. Thus in the *Politics*[8] Aristotle says that the local customs of former times were 'too simple and barbaric'. 'Greeks used to go around armed with swords, and they used to buy wives from one another: and there are certainly other ancient customs that are extremely stupid. In general, all human beings seek not the way of their ancestors, but the good.'

We can then, from within a society or culture and without invoking some kind of higher moral law, come to see that the

---

[7] I rely here on Martha Nussbaum's excellent book on Aristotle's ethics, *The Fragility of Goodness*, Cambridge University Press, 1986, and her essay 'Non-relative Virtues: An Aristotelian Approach', in Martha Nussbaum and Amartya Sen eds., *The Quality of Life*, Oxford, Clarendon Press, 1993.   [8] 1268a39.

ostentatious carrying of weapons in everyday life is a simple-minded relic of earlier 'heroic' ways of life dominated by military virtues, and that treating women as though they were items of barter and commerce is also a relic of a more primitive stage of human culture characterised by human inequality. Both may have been part of the 'way of our ancestors' in the past, but. that is irrelevant; we ought to be concerned with behaviour that makes human beings more fully human. Our ethical 'principles' are tentatively and gradually formed in this way from our reflections on our concrete moral experience, very much as, to use an analogy, in the 'common law' tradition, legal principles are built up on the basis of past judicial decisions which function as 'precedents'. As it has been put, we:

> have a nuclei of experience around which the constructions of different societies proceed. There is no Archimedean point here, no pure access to unsullied 'nature' – even, here, human nature – as it is and of itself. There is just human life as it is lived. But in life as it is lived, we do find a family of experiences, clustering around certain focuses, which can provide reasonable starting points for cross-cultural reflection.[9]

From this point of view, the recognition of universal values can take place within the realm of local knowledge or, put in another way, local knowledge can become self-critical and, like Aristotle's Greeks, stand in judgment on itself.

In parenthesis, it is worth noting that some anti-foundationalists sometimes speak as though local 'contexts or situations or paradigms or communities' functioned as some kind of foundation or absolute point of reference in relation to which the various forms of local knowledge can be judged. Having ushered foundationalism out the front door they surreptitiously bring it in again through the back door. Thus, they speak as though what Stanley Fish calls 'interpretive communities' were well-defined and tightly coherent entities which can speak with a clear and unambiguous voice in particular areas of local knowledge – ethics, the law, religion, science, literature and the arts etc. (We shall see later how some Christian biblical exegetes have exaggerated the coherence of the early Christian communities.) One cannot but be amazed at the

---

[9] Nussbaum, 'Non-Relative Virtues', p. 265.

confidence and ease with which some proponents of local knowledge are able to identify 'the community' and its interpretations.

But, at any one time, there are many sub-communities with conflicting interpretive voices about particular areas of local knowledge, and also conflicting theories or meta-views about foundations and the role of interpretive communities. Any 'consensus' that emerges from this play of forces is always fragile and always contested. Nevertheless, though fragile, this kind of consensus can be real, as already remarked, in the development of the law.

Once again, an analogy with language is helpful here. A language is clearly a human and historical and cultural construct and it is useless (despite Heidegger's playful claim that German was *the* metaphysical language *par excellence*) to attempt to show that it is founded on some kind of universal and necessary and self-justifying rock. But that does not mean that one cannot express universal and necessary truths in a local language, and it does not mean that local languages are incommensurable so that no translation is possible between them. In other words, the recognition that English and Basque are different linguistic systems within two very different socio-cultural contexts does not mean that we cannot say that a sentence in English 'means the same as' a sentence in Basque. Although there are practical limits to translation, it is always possible in principle: indeed translatability is part and parcel of what we mean by a language.

We realise, of course, that translation from one language into another does not imply that there is some kind of supra-linguistic Archimedean or God-like vantage point which enables us to see that a sentence in English means the same as a sentence in Basque. There is no universal language or 'language of the Gods' over and above the local languages! There is only language (in all its human and cultural contingency) and any translation has to be done *within* the respective local languages.

A further point: any language – any linguistic 'tradition' – is open-ended and 'generative', that is it undergoes ceaseless modification and change, sometimes quite radical, and it allows the possibility of new and unpredictable meanings being generated within it. There are, of course, continual attempts to foundationalise language by trying to formalise it and to purify ordinary language of its supposed confusion and ambiguity and 'corruptions'. But the formalist's dream of inventing a perfect language which would bear its meaning clearly and unambiguously upon its face (so that local interpretation is no longer necessary) is simply another form of fundamentalism. At the same time, despite their lack of any kind of Cartesianism foundation, local languages 'work' and we do not, in fact, fall into semiological anarchism or relativism.

THE CONCEPT OF TRADITION

With these philosophical clarifications in mind we can, at last, look more closely at the issue of religious traditions. The concept of tradition has always been an integral part of religious thought and also, of course, of political thought, but it has played a relatively minor role in western philosophical thought, at least until recently.[10] The notion of 'tradition' is, of course, an extremely vague one. It may mean simply received ways or customs ('folkways') of belief and action in a particular community or society, or in a whole culture, and it appeals to a past historical heritage – the 'way of the ancestors' – and acts as a conservative and backward-looking force. But tradition may also have a more creative and forward-looking (and even critical and anti-conservative) meaning as when we use the term of an artistic tradition, or of a philosophical or religious tradition: here a tradition provides distinctive perspectives and paradigms, or models of thought and practice, and generates a 'discourse' of its own.

Again, traditions may be quite particular and local in that they are the tradition of a small and restricted group; or they may be more regional in that they belong to a society or to a whole culture or belief system. These latter are still 'local' in that they do not pretend to global universality (to speak of a global or universal tradition has an air of paradox) but they are not local in any particular sense.

Thus, to use Christianity as an example: there are the traditions

[10] Two exceptions are Michael Polanyi and Alasdair MacIntyre. See the latter's *After Virtue: A Study in Moral Theory*, University of Notre Dame Press, 1981, ch. 15, 'The Virtues, the Unity of a Human Life and the Concept of a Tradition'.

of particular local church communities (as in the case of the early church communities at Corinth or Ephesus); then there are the traditions of different ecclesiastical regions within Christianity such as the Latin or western church as against the eastern church, and, within the western church, the tradition of the Roman Catholic Church as against the traditions of the Reformed Churches and of the Anglican Church. There are also the traditions of cultural regions: thus the Christian traditions of many South American countries are very different from those of most European and English-speaking countries.

To get to grips with the role of tradition in religion it may be helpful once again to focus on one religion, Christianity, and one particular religion, Roman Catholicism. As we shall see, the notion of tradition arises in a peculiarly dramatic way in the Roman Catholic Church, and theological discussion about the role of tradition has been more intense in that church than in most other Christian churches.

In pre-Reformation Christian theology, scripture and an extra-scriptural 'unwritten' tradition were seen as the two main sources of revelation, but the relationship between the two was left unresolved.[11] After the Reformation, scripture alone (*sola scriptura*) came to be seen as the source of Christian revelation, although Reformation theologians understood the idea of 'scripture' in different ways. Luther saw scripture as *interpreted* scripture and was concerned to propose a 'single exegetical tradition of interpreted scripture' as against the prevailing Roman Catholic two sources theory which posited 'an extra-biblical oral tradition' complementing the biblical or scriptural source.[12] Other Reformation and post-Reformation theologians, however, saw 'scripture' in a more literalist way as though the words of the Bible carried their meaning on their face. In any event, the notion of tradition fell into disfavour.

According to Congar, it was only in the nineteenth century that

---

[11] See Yves Congar, *Tradition and Traditions: An Historical and a Theological Essay*, London, 1966.

[12] See H. A. Oberman, *The Dawn of the Reformation: Essays in Late Medieval and Early Reformation Thought*, Edinburgh, T. & T. Clark, 1986, p. 280. See also D. P. Minns 'The Appeal to Tradition and Irenaeus of Lyons', in *Tradition and Traditions*, in *Prudentia*, Supplementary Volume, 1994, University of Newcastle, pp. 79–90.

the idea of tradition was rediscovered in the Roman Catholic Church, mainly through the work of the Tübingen theologian Johann Adam Moehler, though later in the century biblical studies began to focus on the historical formation of the Christian scriptures and the local contexts and church communities within which they were composed. As a result, the concept of tradition was dramatically enlarged; it was no longer merely the repository of unwritten or oral teachings thought to derive from the Apostles, but a kind of condition or presupposition of scripture itself. For Moehler, tradition is bound up with the operation of the Holy Spirit in the church and it is seen as a dynamic principle which brings about new developments in doctrine and the understanding of scripture and also in the life of the Christian community.[13]

From the point of view of historically based scripture studies, the Christian scriptures were composed within local and regional church communities with their own traditions (and their own theological styles) and the scriptural canon was established by reference to those same communities. In fact, Jesus' own teaching and 'way', as a variety of reformed Judaism, was itself formed and elaborated within the context of Judaic tradition as it was in his own time. It would have made no sense outside that tradition. As the Anglican theologian, Stephen Sykes, has said: Jesus did not found Christianity: it 'was founded by Jesus' earliest followers on the foundation of his transformation of Judaism'.[14]

Again, the meaning of scripture was interpreted by reference to the lived experience of the church communities and its general shape and form was continually refined and determined within the same context. If we define 'tradition' in this broad sense as encompassing the lived experience of the church communities and as providing the setting for the composition of the scriptural texts and establishing the scriptural canon, then we can say that tradition makes scripture possible. In other words, scripture does not, and cannot, establish its own credentials or its own privileged canonical status, and it does not bear its meaning upon its face. It

[13] See Congar, *Tradition and Traditions*, pp. 193–6.
[14] Stephen Sykes, *The Identity of Christianity*, Philadelphia, Westminster Press, 1984, p. 20. See also James D. G. Dunn, *Universality and Diversity in the New Testament: An Inquiry into the Character of Earliest Christianity*, London, SCM Press, 1977.

presupposes tradition in the sense that Jesus' revelation, through his preaching and ministry and life and death, was received by communities of believers and interpreted by them and, as was said before, certain writings about Jesus' teaching and life were endowed with privileged status. Further, this process of reception and interpretation of Jesus' revelation continues and 'develops' within local and regional church communities.

Once again, although I have been speaking here of Christianity, analogous remarks can be made of the other 'religions of the Book' – Judaism and Islam – and also of other religious systems like Hinduism and Buddhism which to some extent rely on sacred texts, although in a very different way from Christianity.

THE DEVELOPMENT OF DOCTRINE

The notion of tradition in Christianity is, of course, intimately bound up with the idea of the 'development' of revelation or of believers' understanding of revelation. Earlier views saw the 'deposit' of revelation as being fixed and unalterable: all the truths of Christianity were there in the scriptures (as the Reformers claimed) or in the scriptures and tradition (as the Roman Catholic Church claimed) and nothing could be added to them. But it is obvious that there have been many changes and additions, both in doctrine and practice, in the Christian churches. This is particularly obvious in the case of theological explications of the data of revelation where the latent or implicit content was clarified and 'developed', often through the use of philosophical concepts such as, for example, 'substance' and 'person' and 'nature'. The early twentieth-century French church historian, Louis Duchesne, wrote in 1903 to Alfred Loisy that it was not likely 'that, at his first meeting with St Andrew and St Peter, Our Lord presented them with a visiting card which said, "Jesus Christ, the Eternal Word consubstantial with the Father". Considerable development may be, and is, allowed.'[15] At all events, from the nineteenth century onwards, theologians began to formulate theories about the development of Christian doctrine.[16] One of the earliest and most

---

[15] Cited in Alfred Loisy, *Mémoires pour servir à l'histoire de notre temps*, Paris, Nourry, 3 vols., 1930–1, vol. II, pp. 191–2.

celebrated studies was Newman's *Essay on the Development of Christian Doctrine*, which first appeared in 1845 and then in revised version in 1878. After Newman, the idea of doctrinal development became a central theological topic, and there is a long line of Christian thinkers who have contributed to the debate in the Roman Catholic Church, the Anglican Church, the Reformed Churches and the Orthodox Churches.[17]

The central problem which all the theories of development address is well put by an American Catholic theologian, John Courtney Murray.

That development has taken place . . . cannot possibly be denied. The question is, *what* is legitimate development, what is organic growth in the understanding of the original deposit of faith, what is warranted extension of the primitive doctrine of the church, and what, on the other hand, is accretion, additive increment, adulteration of the deposit, distortion of true Christian discipline? Perhaps, above all, the question is, What are the limits of development and growth – the limits that must be reached on peril of archaistic stuntedness, and the limits that must not be transgressed on peril of futuristic decadence?[18]

Within the Roman Catholic Church, a theological consensus emerged that authentic development was a making explicit of what was implicit in the original deposit of faith, and that this occurred through historical memory in the church recalling certain truths (for example, about the supremacy of the Bishop of Rome), through the logical working out of the implications of basic theological truths (for example, the doctrine of the Trinity), and through the spiritual life of the members of the church witnessing in practice to certain truths (for example, to the special place and status of the Mother of God). The convergence of these three sources of development was, so to speak, ratified by the church's teaching office with 'its sure charism of truth'. As it has been said:

[16] See Aidan Nichols, *From Newman to Congar: The Idea of Doctrinal Development from the Victorians to the Second Vatican Council*, Edinburgh, T. & T. Clark, 1990.

[17] Ibid.; J. Pelikan, *Development of Christian Doctrine: Some Historical Prolegomena*, New Haven, Yale University Press, 1969; O. Chadwick, *From Bossuet to Newman*, Cambridge, Cambridge University Press, 1987; I. Ker, *John Henry Newman: A Biography*, Oxford, Clarendon Press, 1989; Ross Chambers, 'Tradition in Nineteenth Century Russian Orthodox Thought', in *Tradition and Traditions*, in *Prudentia*, 1994, pp. 91–111.

[18] John Courtney Murray, S. J., *The Problem of God Yesterday and Today*, New Haven, Yale University Press, 1964, p. 53.

'The Church's teaching office, with its charism of infallibility, can discern and declare that this convergence has taken place by means of the Holy Spirit, and not from purely human causes.'[19] In this view, the main agent of doctrinal development is the complex life and activity and reflection of the church as a whole – the spiritual practices of the faithful, the speculations of theologians, new insights within the church provoked by social and cultural and political realities and experiences, the pastoral practices of the bishops and other church ministers. The teaching authority of the pope comes into play only when all these sources of development have done their work, and it is limited to discernment and declaration that they derive from the Holy Spirit working in the church. As Karl Rahner observes: 'The Pope is the point at which the collective consciousness of the whole Church attains effective awareness, in a manner which is authoritative for the individual member of the Church.'[20]

In passing, it might also be noted that this conception of the definitive teaching authority of the Pope – the 'magisterium' – is itself a (controversial) 'development' which has emerged relatively recently from within the tradition of the Roman Catholic Church. The nineteenth-century Pope Pius IX is said to have remarked '*I* am tradition' ('La tradizione son'io') meaning that it was the pope who in the last resort defined what was in accordance with tradition and what was not. But, in fact, the present conception of the role of the pope has its source in (recent) tradition. In other words, Pius IX's conception of his authority was the creature of tradition!

The 'collective consciousness of the whole Church' is empha-sised in a statement by the Dutch Catholic bishops in 1960. For the bishops, the church is essentially a community and the develop-ment of doctrine and of the life of faith within the church is a work of the whole community. Various ideas, influences, attitudes form within the Christian community and

by a continual process of confrontation and purification, in which all the faithful play their part – sacramental practices, popular devotions,

---

[19] Nichols, *From Newman to Congar*, p. 264.
[20] *Theological Investigations*, vol. 4, 1966, p. 34.

ecclesiastical movements, theological research, the intellectual talents of such and such a people, different outlooks between the laity and the clergy – all these factors contribute to the life of faith. In this gradual fermentation, foreign elements are gradually eliminated and the theological formulation finds an adequate expression of what was always in the Church implicitly. We are led then to recognise a collective conception formed by the whole community of faith, and this conception is infallible, not only in principle but also in fact. 'The faith of the Universal Church . . . cannot be deceived', says St Thomas, formulating the opinion of the whole tradition of faith.[21]

At the Second Vatican Council this consensus was enshrined (in more restrained terms) in the *Dogmatic Constitution on Divine Revelation, (Dei Verbum)*.

The Tradition that comes from the apostles makes progress in the Church with the help of the Holy Spirit. There is a growth in insight into the realities and words that are being passed on. This comes about in various ways. It comes through the contemplation and study of believers who ponder these things in their hearts. It comes from the intimate sense of spiritual realities which they experience. And it comes from the preaching of those who have received, along with their right of succession in the episcopate, the sure charism of truth. Thus, as the centuries go by, the Church is always moving towards the plenitude of divine truth, until eventually the words of God are fulfilled in her.[22]

The development of doctrine within the church is then largely the work of tradition, taken in its widest sense as the lived experience of the whole church community both in the past and the present. And, if we understand tradition as the operation of various forms of 'local knowledge' in particular and regional communities within the church, and not as some kind of Cartesian foundation, we can then appreciate the importance of local knowledge in Christianity. The reception and interpretation of Jesus' original revelation take place with regard to it, the canon of sacred scriptures is constituted by reference to it, and the development of Christian doctrine has its main source in it.

The notion of the development of Christian doctrine that has been described here is an idealised one. There have been many

---

[21] *Catholic Documentation*, 6, no. 4, September, 1961.
[22] *Dogmatic Constitution on Divine Revelation*, ch. 11, section 8, in Walter M. Abbott, ed., *The Documents of Vatican 11*, London, Geoffrey Chapman, 1966, p. 116.

'official' developments in doctrine in the Roman Catholic Church, especially concerning Christian morality, which have not followed the complex formal process we have been discussing. Again, for this notion of development to have practical or operational meaning, from time to time it must be possible in some way to discern a recognisable and coherent tendency in, and a convergence of, Christian devotional life, theological discussion and pastoral teaching and practice, of the kind described. But, as Rahner has pointed out in his later writings, the pluralism that characterises the modern world has also radically affected Catholic theology and life itself, so that it is not longer really practicable to think that there can be a common theology or a recognisable *sensus fidelium* that might give rise to 'a collective conception formed by the whole community of faith' and that might provide the basis for a new doctrinal development. 'Today', Rahner says,

a pluralism exists in regional cultures, philosophies, terminologies, outlooks, theologies, and so on, which can no longer be reduced to any one synthesis, and so vividly has the Church become aware of this that I can no longer imagine that any specific, and at the same time genuinely new, proposition can be expressed that can be felt so thoroughly to be an expression of the common faith of the whole Church as to be capable of definition.[23]

But, in a sense, Rahner's assumption that this is an entirely new phenomenon and that the past was radically different, is questionable. In actual practice, Roman Catholic theology in the past was, despite the church's public rhetoric about the unity and continuity of doctrine and discipline, almost as pluralistic as it is at present. Again, the exercise of the 'sure charism of truth' by the teaching authority or magisterium of the Roman Catholic Church has on occasion proved to be notably unsure and fallible. It would be interesting to draw up a balance sheet of the Catholic magisterium's wins and losses in its various interventions in matters of faith and morals, and it is not at all clear that the result would be a favourable one. Thus, as an ironic example, the present Catholic notions of tradition and of the development of doctrine, adopted by

---

[23] Karl Rahner, 'The Concept of Infallibility in Catholic Theology', in *Theological Investigations*, 14, 1976, 72–3.

the Second Vatican Council, were rejected by the Council of Trent and the First Vatican Council and by a number of nineteenth-century papal statements. Equally, formal statements of the magisterium in the nineteenth century apropos the interpretation of the scriptures showed, in the light of subsequent developments in the church, how unsure these exercises of the 'sure charism of truth' were. Further, a great many of the church's swingeing censures of the Modernist movement in the late nineteenth century have been, in effect, countermanded by later official pronouncements. The endorsement of religious freedom of conscience in the Second Vatican Council's *Declaration on Human Freedom* is a notable example of this.[24] (Any serious account of the 'infallibility' of the magisterium has to take into account that on very many issues the magisterium got it wrong, so that we can only speak of the infallibility of the church or the magisterium in a very broad and qualified sense, namely, that, in general and on balance and taking a long view, the theological direction of the church will prove in the fullness of time, despite various aberrations, to have been right.)

We rejoin here the remarks made before on the tendency for some anti-foundationalists to reintroduce foundationalist ideas by speaking as though interpretive communities can speak in a clear and decisive voice in the particular areas of local knowledge. In the post Counter Reformation period, the Roman Catholic Church, having rejected scriptural fundamentalism (where the text of the scriptures was itself deemed to be self-justifying), developed a form of institutional fundamentalism in the guise of a contestable version of papal infallibility and of the church's teaching authority or magisterium. Just as for the scriptural fundamentalist the literal text of the scriptures (the 'word of God') bears its meaning on its face and does not need to be interpreted, so for the institutional fundamentalist the decisions of the magisterium are self-justifying and do not need to be interpreted. by reference to tradition.[25] A Christian believes that the unity and continuity of the church and the complex processes of doctrinal development are being guided by the Holy Spirit and that believers have a right to be hopeful that

---

[24] *Declaration on Human Freedom*, in W. M. Abbott ed., *The Documents of Vatican II*.

[25] See Bruno Neveu, *L'erreur et son juge. Remarques sur les censures doctrinales à l'époque moderne*, Naples, Bibliopolis, 1993.

the church will not collapse into anarchic sectarianism in the future. But one has no right to expect that this guidance will operate in a *miraculous* way and that we will be able to see *evidently* that the process is being guided by the Holy Spirit. As Rahner says, the best we can expect is that it will all be shown to have a meaning 'at the end of things'.

The conclusion of this discussion of tradition in the Roman Catholic Church is that tradition, in the extended sense in which we have used it, is the main constitutive principle in the teaching and practice and life of the church. This is a paradoxical finding, given the Roman Catholic Church's 'official' emphasis upon the universal (non-local) character of its teaching and upon its strongly centralised view of the church and of its teaching authority or magisterium. However, it is also a finding in tune with many developments that are taking place in the Roman Catholic Church at the grass-roots or 'unofficial' level – the recognition that the church is primarily a human community and not a juridical structure, the interest in 'basic Christian communities', the emphasis on the 'inculturation' of the Gospel, the fostering of 'creative dissent' within the church, the acceptance of pluralism in society at large and in Christian theology and practice.

CONCLUSIONS

Is it possible to discern analogies between the history of the universal and local elements in the Roman Catholic Church and similar developments first in other Christian churches, and then in other religious systems? I have argued that the universal and local elements are, philosophically speaking, necessary features of religion as such (just as they are of ethics as such) in that, on the one hand, any religion must make supra-local or universal truth claims, and, on the other hand, any religion must be practised in a local situation or context. From this point of view, there *must* be analogies between the various religious traditions, and it must be possible to classify religions in terms of the balance they strike between the universalising and localising tendencies.

Some religious traditions will emphasise the universal aspect and lay great stress on establishing and maintaining the original revelation while being suspicious of, and devaluing, the local element. Other traditions will de-emphasise the universal element and focus on the creativity and vitality and openness to the Spirit that springs from a living local tradition. At one end of the spectrum one could place a highly institutionalised religious tradition like the Roman Catholic Church (or, rather, the contemporary form of 'official' Roman Catholicism) and, to a certain extent, Judaism and Islam. In these religions 'orthodoxy' (right belief) is central. At the other end of the spectrum one might place Buddhism and Taoism and other religions where there is a very attenuated institutional structure and where 'orthopraxy' (right action and practice) is all important.

In a remarkable study, the French religious sociologist, Jean Claude Galey, has shown how, in Hinduism, local practices about important pilgrimages involving a number of particular local sites are related to the universal themes of Hinduism. Whereas the function of the cult of saints in the Latin part of the Christian Church is to relate a local story to a non-local or universal centre, so that the local cult only has meaning through that relation, the function of pilgrimages in India is, on the contrary, to import universal themes into the local sites involved in the particular pilgrimages. The pilgrimage 'makes the particular the very condition of the expression and realisation of the universal'. In general, 'Hinduism endows each of the ensemble of [pilgrimage] sites with the capacity to be the expression of its fundamental representations and so to transform each locality into a nucleus of high [religious] density.'[26]

One must not press cross-cultural comparisons too closely, but there is an analogy between Galey's view of Indian pilgrimages and the beliefs and practices of certain Australian Aboriginal groups concerning the Ancestor Spirits. These beings (not to be confused with gods) shaped both the cosmos and local territories or 'countries' 'at the beginning of things' and, on their mythical wanderings and adventures, left their life-force and spiritual power in certain 'sacred sites'. Maintaining and caring for those local sites and drawing on their spiritual power is a major religious task. In

[26] Jean Claude Galey, 'L'universel dans la localité. Implications sociologiques du pélerinage en Inde', *Revue de l'histoire des religions*, 211, July-September, 1994, 261–2.

this sense the universal realities of Australian Aboriginal religions expressed in the great foundation myths are made present and operative in and through the local sacred sites.[27]

At various stages in its history a religion may go through different phases, so that at one time the localising tendency may be dominant, and at another time the universalising tendency may prevail. Since the Counter Reformation, the Roman Catholic Church has tended to emphasise the universal aspect and to see localising tendencies as dangerous to the identity and continuity of the original revelation. But, at least at the grassroots or unofficial level, there are signs that the local element will become more dominant. One can detect similar oscillations within Hinduism and even in Buddhism.

How can we judge the value of particular religious traditions? Believers in the various traditions will, of course, point to the truth of the original revelation around which the tradition formed, and to the historical continuity between the original revelation and what is believed and practised now. Others will place more emphasis on the creative aspects of their tradition and see it as a source of personal holiness and of social concern for human liberation in all its dimensions. ('By their fruits shall you know them'.) For these latter it is important not merely to safeguard and preserve the original revelation, but to open it up and develop it. A tradition ought both to maintain old things and to bring new things to birth: *et nova et vetera*. The vitality and fecundity of a religious tradition and its capacity to give rise to genuine developments are criteria which can be seen as analogous to those applicable to literary and artistic traditions, and, as has already been noted, it can be illuminating to see a religious tradition on the model of a literary or artistic tradition such as, for example, the tradition of Romanticism or of Impressionism.

Throughout this discussion, I have been insisting that both the universal element and the local element are essential in religion, even though most of the discussion has been about the local element. It has been necessary to clarify the idea of local knowledge

---

[27] On the importance of local sites in certain Australian Aboriginal religions see Tony Swain, *A Place for Strangers: Towards a History of Australian Aboriginal Being*, Cambridge University Press, 1993.

and to defend it against various misunderstandings (both of some of its proponents and its enemies) and to assert its importance. In particular, it has been argued that criticism of Cartesian foundationalism and emphasis on local knowledge does not necessarily end in relativism or, in the religious sphere, in sectarianism. Again, the philosophical debate about anti-foundationalism has been shown to have important implications for the notion of religious tradition, particularly in Roman Catholic theology, but also generally. However, while the focus has been on local knowledge (and tradition) both the local element and the universal element are necessary in any religion: here, as elsewhere, it is the balance that is everything. That is, of course, a truism but it is a significant truism.

The making of a Christian ethics

CAN THERE BE A CHRISTIAN ETHICS?

The question of whether there can be a distinctively Christian ethics is now a well-worn one, and it might be thought that nothing very original can be said about it. In European and English and American theology there is a sharp division between those who believe that there is indeed a distinctive and autonomous Christian ethics, and, on the other hand, those who think that, while a Christian religious commitment provides a special moral perspective and motivation, there is, in fact, no Christian ethics providing the basis for specific ethical norms and a specific ethical methodology. Within the two camps there are important differences, and a spectrum of positions has developed on both sides.

While I attempt to show that the idea of an autonomous Christian ethics is philosophically untenable and so align myself with those who reject an 'ethics of belief' (*Glaubensethik*, as some German theologians call it), my main interest here is in the way the idea of a Christian ethic has been used in the elaboration of a moral theology or theory about the Christian life.

The thesis of this essay may be expressed in a schematic way as follows:

The basic ethical principles must be accessible to all human beings who are rationally competent (the term 'rational' is used in the widest and most neutral sense) since a contradiction would be involved in human beings being obliged to follow certain ethical imperatives and, on the other hand, being unable to know – at least in principle – what those imperatives were.

The ethical precepts contained in the Christian revelation (and, for that matter, in all religious revelations) are not accessible to all human beings since they apply only to, and have meaning for, those who have a knowledge of and religious commitment to (or faith in) that revelation. Even if we claimed (dubiously) that, in principle at least, the Christian revelation is now accessible to all human beings throughout the world, that was certainly not the case for all those human beings who lived before the coming of Jesus Christ two thousand years ago.

The ethical precepts contained specifically within the Christian revelation may partially complement, but cannot replace, the rationally based ethical principles which apply to all human beings as human beings, and they are not sufficient to provide a systematic and comprehensive body of ethical teaching. In this sense there is not, and cannot be, a 'Christian ethics' which has a distinctive method and content and which is, so to speak, in competition with other ethical systems which are the result of human enquiry. Of course, there is a body of ethical teaching derived from human enquiry which is consonant with, or in general harmony with, the Christian view of the world and human affairs, and in this very loose sense there can be a 'Christian ethics'. But all the elements of that body of ethical teaching originate, as has been said, from human enquiry. As the American Reformed theologian, James T. Gustafson, has put it: 'Christian action-guiding values and principles can be inferred from religious belief as normative for those who share some common Christian experience of the reality of God.' But this 'religious qualification of morality does not create an exclusive morality or ethics'.

To use an analogy: if this argument is correct, there cannot be a systematic and universal 'Christian ethics' any more than there can be a systematic 'Christian philosophy', as distinct from a body of philosophical teaching which is in general harmony with Christian belief. Many different philosophical positions are in harmony with Christian belief and no one position is, so to speak, more privileged than another; the same is true of the various different ethical positions which are consonant with the Christian way of life.

We can then distinguish between, on the one hand, what we might call the ethics of Christian revelation with its ideal prescriptions about the way of Christian perfection, and addressed principally to Christian believers, and, on the other hand, the ethics based on human enquiry and addressed to all human agents. While we cannot neatly separate the two 'ethics', it is important to distinguish between them because there are opportunities for confusion in both directions. Thus, on the one hand, the ideal prescriptions of Jesus for the life of perfection and addressed to believers might be seen as standard ethical obligations applying to all: some theologians, for example, claim that Jesus' teaching on marriage has been misinterpreted in just this way. And, on the other hand, the standard prescriptions of the ethics of human enquiry might be given the status of divinely sanctioned commands as though they were part of God's revelation to be believed by religious faith. As we shall see, an attempt has been made in Roman Catholic moral theology to make the prescriptions of 'natural law' into quasi-infallible 'truths of revelation'.

Two consequences follow from the discussion above: first, the claim by the Christian churches to have elaborated a systematic and universal and independent Christian ethics cannot be sustained; the best they can claim is that, through human enquiry, they have developed a body of ethical teaching which is generally consonant with the values implicit in the Gospels. If this is true, those churches which claim to be divinely authorised teachers of a universal Christian ethics clearly have to reinterpret their role.

Second, the discipline of moral theology which has been created within certain Christian churches (in particular the Roman Catholic Church) has a much more modest domain, and more diminished importance, than is at present claimed for it. Some years ago, the English theologian, John Mahoney, wrote an admirable book entitled *The Making of Moral Theology*[1] in which he showed the development of moral theology in the Roman Catholic Church as resulting almost from a process of Heath Robinson 'bricolage'. This present essay, on the other hand, might be entitled 'the deconstruction of moral theology' in that it recalls the

[1] Oxford, Clarendon Press, 1987. See also Vincent McNamara, *Faith and Ethics: Recent Roman Catholicism*, Dublin, Gill, 1985, and Charles E. Curran and Richard A. McCormick eds., *Readings in Moral Theology*, ch. 2, 'The Distinctiveness of Christian Ethics', New Jersey, Paulist Press, 1980.

discipline to its real and central task, namely the explication of the Christian 'way of perfection'.

In a survey of Catholic theology at mid-century, the great Belgian theologian, Roger Aubert, after lamenting the legalism and sterility of much current moral theology, claimed that moral theology must henceforth see morality 'presented as the Christian's answer to the call of Christ, the generous response of a person to the ennobling call of another Person'.[2] Again, in an essay written after the Second Vatican Council, the eminent Catholic moral theologian, Josef Fuchs, argued that moral theology must be centrally concerned with 'the perfection of consciences under the personal and individual guidance of the Holy Spirit'.[3] These remarks are very much in line with the theme of this essay, though one would have to admit that their authors' hopes have, alas, yet to be realised.

IDEALISTIC PERFECTIONISM

Jesus' Sermon on the Mount, reported in Matthew's gospel (5–7), is commonly seen as the quintessence of his ethical or moral teaching, in so far as that can be distinguished from the example of his life. In a sense it presupposes the broad ethical principles of the Jewish Law – that people should not kill others, commit adultery, swear false oaths, take revenge, treat their neighbours as enemies. But the point of Jesus' sermon is that while his followers should certainly keep these basic ethical prescriptions, they should also go beyond them and practice them in a 'perfect' way. For his followers it is not sufficient that they do not kill, or commit adultery or take revenge: his followers should not even be angry with others (5. 21–6); they should not even have lustful desires (5. 27–30); they should not even defend themselves but 'turn the other cheek' (5. 43–7) and love their enemies.

[2] R. Aubert, *La Théologie catholique au milieu du XXe siècle*, Paris, 1954, p. 8. See also William J. O'Brien ed., *Riding Time Like a River: The Catholic Moral Tradition Since Vatican II*, Washington, Georgetown University Press, 1993. See especially ch. 5, John R. Donahue, 'The Challenge of the Biblical Renewal to Moral Theology', and ch. 6, John Mahoney, 'Conscience, Discernment and Prophecy in Moral Decision Making'.

[3] Josef Fuchs, *Human Values and Christian Morality*, Dublin, Gill, p. 34.

Jesus' ethical or moral teaching has been characterised as 'idealistic perfectionism' and 'prophetic radicality'[4] because its precepts go beyond accepted moral teaching and require not just virtue but 'heroic' or supererogatory virtue, not just doing what we are obliged to do, but going beyond the call of duty or obligation. To use a later (and to some degree, unfortunate) description, its teaching is primarily concerned with 'counsels of perfection'. In a sense, the rich young man in Matthew's Gospel (19. 16–22) represents the main audience Jesus wished to address.

In parenthesis, while the Christian way of perfection is concerned with 'obligations' which go beyond ordinary ethical obligations, they are not supererogatory in the sense that the Christian believer can take them or leave them as he or she chooses. As Max Weber said of the Sermon on the Mount: 'This ethics is no joking matter. The same holds for this ethics as has been said of causality in science: it is not a cab which one can have stopped at one's pleasure: it is all or nothing.'[5]

From this point of view, Jesus was not concerned to put forward a comprehensive ethical system of the kind that the great Greek thinkers -Plato, Aristotle, the Stoic philosophers, the Epicureans – had adumbrated three hundred years before. Jesus accepted the main ethical precepts of the Judaism of his time (although he rejected certain of the interpretations of that body of teaching) which were inextricably bound up with religious ritual observances and taboos, ceremonial rules, social conventions and customs, dietary rules etc. All were seen as part of the seamless web of the Law given by God to the Jewish people, and all were justified, so to speak, by appeal to the God of the Jewish scriptures. Strictly speaking, these precepts applied only to those who believed in that God and who belonged to the House of Israel, and they were not meant to have universal import, as though they applied to all

---

[4] See E. P. Sanders, *The Historical Figure of Jesus*, London, Allen Lane, Penguin Press, 1993, p. 201; also see Norbert Greinacher, 'Zur Problem von Scheidunge und Wiederverheiratung', *Theologische Quartalschrift*, 167:2, 1987, 106. English summary in *Theology Digest*, 35, 1988, 222. A good overview is provided by J. Lambrecht, *The Sermon on the Mount: Proclamation and Exhortation*, Wilmington, Del., Glazier, 1988.

[5] Max Weber, 'Politics as a Vocation', in H. H. Gewirth and C. Wright Mills eds., *From Max Weber: Essays in Sociology*, London, Routledge and Kegan Paul, 1948, p. 119.

human beings whether they were Jewish or not. The Israelites were, by divine definition, a select or 'chosen' group, and their Law applied primarily to that small elect group of human beings.

In this scheme of things the position of the Gentiles or non-Jews was, in a sense, paradoxical. It was recognised that they could behave ethically or morally, at least at a basic level, but, since they were outside the Law, they were *ipso facto* 'wicked' or 'sinners'. As E. P. Sanders has put it:

The Jews who translated the Hebrew Bible into Greek . . . used the word 'sinners' (*harmartoloi*) and this became the term that Greek-speaking Jews used for people who were fundamentally outside the covenant because they did not observe God's law. The word 'sinners' in Jewish Greek could refer to Gentiles (who by definition did not observe the Jewish law) or to truly wicked Jews.[6]

In much the same way Jesus' 'idealistic perfectionism' was not meant to have universal import and meaning for all human beings. His 'way' was meant only for those who had made a religious commitment to him and accepted him as 'the way, the truth and the life' and who saw him as the personal realisation of the prophetic prefigurings in the Jewish scriptures. No doubt, Jesus clearly recognised that those Gentiles or non-Jews who had faith in him could participate in his Kingdom – the Roman centurion, the Samaritan woman, the Canaanite mother and other non-Jews reported in the Gospels who display that faith, are moving examples – but he also insisted that his primary mission was to the 'lost sheep of the House of Israel'.[7] However, even when, after Jesus' death, the Christian church communities became more and more open to the Gentiles and Christianity was no longer seen as a reform movement within Judaism, the ethical teaching of the church was not seen as having universal application. Just as the Jewish Law applied only to those who made a religious commitment to the God of the Jewish scriptures, so Jesus' ethical teaching applied only to those who made a religious commitment to him. The ultimate justification of that teaching was that it came from one who had revealed that he was the 'way, the truth and the life'.

---

[6] E. P. Sanders, *The Historical Figure of Jesus*, p. 227.
[7] Matthew 8. 10; 15. 21–8.

In principle Jesus' 'way' was available to everyone, Jew and Gentile, but only if an act of faith in Jesus or a religious commitment were made to him.

By way of summary, we can adopt the view of the American biblical theologian, Wayne A. Meeks, on the Sermon on the Mount in Matthew's Gospel:

Although the risen Jesus in Matthew directs that new disciples must be taught 'to observe all that I have commanded you' (28:20), we have here no system of commandments. The rules are exemplary, not comprehensive, pointers to the kind of life expected in the community, but not a map of acceptable behaviour. Still less does Matthew's Jesus state philosophical principles from which guidelines could rationally be derived.[8]

St Paul takes up very much the same stance, although he is more concerned with the general ethical or moral issues of his time, ranging from anger to drunkenness to homosexuality, jealousy, lying, pederasty, stealing. The various 'vice lists' that St Paul refers to,[9] and in terms of which he admonishes his Christian communities, are mostly taken from current philosophical ethical teaching, especially Stoicism. Vice lists were, in fact, in vogue in popular philosophical circles (Philo, for example, had drawn up a list of 160 vices of the pleasure lover) and there was nothing original in St Paul's own lists.[10] For the most part St Paul is concerned with

---

[8] Wayne A. Meeks, *The Origins of Christian Morality: The First Two Centuries*, New Haven, Yale University Press, 1993, p. 200. For an overview of the vast array of recent scholarly writing on Jesus' ethics see William C. Spohn, 'Jesus and Christian Ethics', *Theological Studies*, 56, 1995, 92–107. See also Lisa Sowle Cahill, *Love Your Enemies: Discipleship, Pacifism and Just War Theory*, Minneapolis, Fortress Press, 1994, pp. 26–9. It is worth noting that for most of the early Middle Ages the moral system taught in western Christianity was based upon the seven deadly or capital sins: Pride, Envy, Wrath, Avarice, Gluttony, Sloth and Lechery. 'The list was not Christian, but Greek and possibly astrological in origin. In its medieval form it had been given authority by Pope Gregory the Great and systematised as part of a larger system of septenary forms of instruction during the twelfth century. It was related to the moral teaching of the New Testament by being treated as a negative exposition of the two commandments of the Gospel, the love of God and the love of one's neighbour': John Bossy, 'Moral Arithmetic: Seven Sins into Ten Commandments', in Edmund Leites ed., *Conscience and Casuistry in Early Modern Europe*, Cambridge University Press, 1988, p. 215.

[9] See Romans 1. 29–31; 13. 13; I Corinthians 5. 10–11; 2 Corinthians 12. 20–21; Galatians, 5. 19–21.

[10] See Jerome Murphy-O'Connor, *Becoming Human Together: The Pastoral Anthropology of St Paul*, Wilmington, Michael Glazier, 1982, pp. 132–5.

fostering the life of the various Christian communities and directing their behaviour.[11]

It was really only with St Augustine that larger claims were made and that the idea of a Christian ethics emerged. So Augustine says; 'In what Scripture expressly affirms is to be found everything we need for our life of faith and our moral life.'[12] However, Augustine forgets that in his own ethical teaching on abortion, justice in warfare, human sexuality, marriage, suicide, lying, the freedom of religious belief and other matters, he draws heavily on extra-scriptural ethical concepts and themes (especially of a quasi-Platonic provenance).[13]

The ethical teachings of both Judaism and Jesus' 'way' were entirely typical of most religious 'ways' which are usually undifferentiated complexes of ritual observances, dietary and pollution taboos, liturgical rules, ancestral customs, calls to 'perfect' or heroic forms of living (involving self-abnegation, poverty, virginity, pacifism etc.) and ethical or moral rules in something like the modern sense. They all depend upon a particular religious commitment and are justified in terms of that commitment.

GREEK ETHICS

We may contrast this kind of ethics with the view of ethics as an independent rational discipline or enquiry of its own disengaged from any religious setting and surroundings and claiming to be both a systematic body of truths and universal in application. This view of ethics was the achievement of the great Greek philosophers, Socrates, Plato, Aristotle, the Stoics and their successors, some 300 years before the advent of Jesus.

It would be wrong to see classical Greek ethics as a form of secularist or naturalistic enquiry opposed to the religious ethics of the various sects. In one sense that is true enough, since for Plato

---

[11] See Meeks, *The Origins of Christian Morality*, p. 201: 'Almost without exception, the documents that eventually became the New Testament and most of the other surviving documents from the same period of Christianity's beginnings are concerned with the way converts to the movement should behave.'   [12] *De doctrina christiana*, 11, 14. PL 39, 42.
[13] See Mahoney, *The Making of Moral Theology*, ch. 2. The uneasy mingling of biblical themes, Roman practices and Greek philosophy in Augustine's 'just war ' theory is well described by Lisa Sowle Cahill, *Love Your Enemies*, ch. 4.

and Aristotle the final justification of an ethical position is a philosophical or rational one based on a consideration of what it is to be human in the fullest sense – to be flourishingly or 'eu-daimonistically' human, as Aristotle would say. But one needs to remember that, for Plato in particular, and for his Neoplatonic heirs, philosophy itself is seen in quasi-religious terms as a way of enlightenment. As Pierre Hadot has reminded us: in the Greek, Hellenistic and Roman view philosophy was understood as

a way of life, which does not mean only that it is a certain moral conduct . . . but that it is a way of existing in the world, which should be practised at each instant and which should transform one's life.[14]

Thus, the great Roman thinker, Seneca, who had an enormous influence on subsequent Christian ethical thinking,[15] saw the rational discipline of philosophy as a way of attaining union with 'the best part of the self' which is identified with the Universal Reason that pervades nature and the cosmos: one becomes 'aware of oneself as part of nature, as a portion of Universal Reason'. In this sense, philosophy is a 'spiritual exercise'.[16] It is obvious that this idea of reason has very little to do with the 'secularist' view of reason (set over against religion) that emerges from the European Enlightenment in the seventeenth century.

Nevertheless, it remains true that the essence of Greek ethics was that ethical rules were, as said before, derived in the last resort from an enquiry into human reality – not into human 'nature' under-stood as a rigidly fixed and unchanging structure, but into what it is to be human in the fullest and richest sense. Further, it was an essential feature of Greek ethics that ethical rules applied univer-sally to all fully rational agents, and not just 'domestically' or parochially to the members of a particular group of religious believers like the Orphic and Pythagorean sects.[17]

Christianity was born into a cultural context where Greek

[14] P. Hadot, *Philosophy as a Way of Life: Spiritual Exercises from Socrates to Foucault*, ed. Arnold I. Davidson, London, Blackwell, 1995, p. 103.

[15] See Gerard Verbeke, *The Presence of Stoicism in Medieval Thought*, Washington, Catholic University of America, 1987.

[16] P. Hadot, 'Reflections on the Idea of the "Cultivation of the Self" ', in *Philosophy as a Way of Life*, p. 207.

[17] On the relationship between Greek religion and morality see Walter Burkert, *Greek Religion*, Cambridge Mass., Harvard University Press, 1985.

philosophy and ethical thinking were an accomplished fact, and eventually Christian thinkers had to come to terms with them, first for apologetical purposes in explaining and defending the Christian message to educated non-Christians, and second for their own theological purposes in explicating and developing Christian doctrine.[18]

However, as we shall see, that interchange between Christianity and Greek philosophy, while useful for Christianity's purposes, also had untoward effects, especially in the realm of the ethics of human sexuality. In particular, it brought about a (selective) conflation between the ethically ideal and the real. For example, an American moral theologian, Lisa Sowle Cahill, has drawn attention to 'a fundamental besetting problem of Catholic teaching about marriage: a conflation of the ideal and the real'. She goes on: 'A picture of marriage as "total" self-gift which could attract and inspire were it held out in the same evangelical mode as Jesus' command to "love your enemies" or "leave all and follow me", becomes oppressive and alienating when it skewers married persons on standards which are not only impossible, but also inequitable in relation to church expectations in other realms of life.'[19] In other words, Jesus' prohibition of divorce was meant as an ideal demand to those of his followers who wished to live a life of 'perfection' – a demand on the same level as 'leave all and follow me' – and not as an absolute ethical.precept imposing a strict obligation on all human beings. That absolutisation and universalisation of a 'counsel of perfection' (making 'heroic virtue' into ordinary virtue) was largely brought about through the influence of Greek ethical thinking on Christianity.

CONTEMPORARY CHRISTIAN ETHICS

Christian ethical teaching is now concerned with quite specific issues, for example about human sexuality and reproduction –

---

[18] On this process in the thought of Clement of Alexandria, Basil the Great, John Chrysostom and Augustine see Eric Osborn, *Ethical Patterns in Early Christian Thought*, Cambridge University Press, 1976.

[19] Lisa Sowle Cahill, 'Marriage', in Michael J. Walsh ed., *Commentary on the Catechism of the Catholic Church*, Collegeville, Minn., The Liturgical Press, 1994, pp. 328–9.

marriage, divorce, homosexuality, reproductive technology and the new forms of assisted reproduction such as *in vitro* fertilisation, contraception ('natural' and artificial) and the use of condoms in the control of HIV/AIDS, abortion, the ethical status of the human embryo, surrogate motherhood. Again, it offers a Christian ethical perspective on quite unprecedented questions raised by the manipulation of the genetic make-up of human beings. It is also concerned with issues about death and dying: the distinction between suicide and legitimately refusing 'burdensome' or 'extra-ordinary' medical treatment even while knowing that this will result in one's death, the allied distinction between actively assisting a person to die and letting a person die. The contemporary Christian ethic also has a strong social dimension in that it proposes views of peace and war, the use of nuclear weapons as a 'deterrent', the ownership of property and the distribution of wealth, the role of the state and the scope of social justice and human liberation, capital punishment, attitudes to the poor and needy, human equality and the position of women. The recently published *Cathechism of the Catholic Church*[20] has, in addition, specified 'new commandments' about, for example, our obligation to pay justly levied taxes, not to pollute the environment, not to overindulge in food or alcohol or tobacco, not to engage in drug-trafficking, kidnapping, taking hostages, terrorism, torture etc.[21]

No doubt, the various Christian churches see this Christian ethic in different ways. At one extreme there is the position of the Roman Catholic Church which is the most explicit, and most floridly detailed and systematic. As we shall see, the Roman Catholic Church relies heavily on an ethical theory based on rational enquiry, the 'natural law' theory, to articulate its position. It also makes the claim (though ambiguously) that the church alone can interpret the true meaning of the 'natural law', even though the latter is a philosophical theory based on human reason and subject to the canons of reason. At the other extreme, there are the Christian churches which reject any attempt to introduce human

---

[20] *Catechism of the Catholic Church*, St Paul, Libreria Editrice Vaticana, 1994.
[21] Ibid. 2290, 2291, 2297. For the wide range of issues now seen as part of 'Christian ethics' see the English journal *Studies in Christian Ethics*. See especially the special issue of the journal, 8:1, 1995, 'Christian Ethics; Modernity and Postmodernity'.

reason into the realm of religious faith. Some claim, with Karl Barth, that the idea of a philosophically based ethics relying on human enquiry apart from Christian revelation is an illusion. The only true ethics is one based upon God's commands. As Barth argues: 'The grace of God protests against every humanly established ethics as such.' And again:

A theological ethic disagrees with all other ethics in so far as the basis and origin of ethics in the command of God is obscured or denied and independent principles for ethics are proposed; a theological ethics cannot take such ethical endeavours seriously.[22]

A vulgarised version of this 'theocratic' position is to be found in forms of American Christian fundamentalism. For the fundamentalists, the various prescriptions to be found in the Bible are to be understood literally and they are to be taken as universal and absolute. The biblical prescriptions constitute a complete ethical system (fundamentalists do not recognise extra-biblical ethical sources) and the state has an obligation to give them legislative expression. 'Fundamentalism', two recent observers say,

represents a current in American life that has always lived side by side with, but in considerable opposition to, the Jeffersonian spirit of openness and questioning of authority. It imposes on all matters a quality of ideological totalism – of insistence of all-or-none judgments and positions.[23]

Others claim, more moderately, that, while one can derive certain ethical norms from within the Christian way of life, those norms apply only to believers in that way of life. Thus Gustafson says:

On the basis of the assumption that certain values and principles have an obligatory character within a 'way of life' and that the Christian history and community call for a way of life grounded in the Christian story, it is fitting to call them Christian ethical principles and values.

But those principles and values do not oblige those who have no commitment to the Christian way of life. 'It is unreasonable to assume that those who do not share the "believing" should be

---

[22] Cited in Paul Lehman, *Ethics in a Christian Context*, London, SCM Press, 1963, pp. 175–6.
[23] Robert Jay Lifton and Charles B. Strozier, *New York Times Book Review*, 12 August 1990, p. 25.

obliged to follow the principles and honor the values that are distinctive to that community'.[24]

Finally, there are those who claim that, while we cannot derive an autonomous Christian ethic from 'gospel values', those values nevertheless provide a distinctive Christian point of view or perspective on ethical issues. Some American Christians, for example, have argued that the spirit of 'democratic capitalism' is consonant with certain gospel values which can be discerned in the scriptures.[25]

However, while there are these differences between the Christian Churches, many of them, as we have noted, speak as though their ethical views have universal reference and import. Indeed, they are so confident of this that they call on the state to ensure that its laws, applying to all members of society and not just to members of the church, should be in conformity with their view of the Christian ethic on issues such as abortion, contraception, assisted reproduction, marriage and divorce and family formation, assisted suicide and so on.

How do we account for this extraordinary change from Jesus' Sermon on the Mount to these new forms of the Christian ethic? How has a statement of 'idealistic perfectionism', meant for a small group of religiously committed believers in Jesus, become a systematic and universalistic body of ethical teaching on a wide range of quite specific ethical issues ranging from the use of condoms in sexual intercourse to the use of nuclear weapons in warfare?

A standard reply is that contemporary ethical teaching and the development of moral theology in the Christian churches is simply the result of detailed extrapolation and working out of the basic ethical values contained in the Gospels *vis-à-vis* the new personal and socio-cultural and economic problems presented by western civilisation and the modern world generally. Dogmatic or system-

---

[24] 'Can Ethics Be Christian?', in Charles E. Curran and Richard A. McCormick eds., *Readings in Moral Theology*, New Jersey, Paulist Press, 1980, vol. II, p. 177. See also Gustafson's book, *Protestant and Roman Catholic Ethics*, London, 1979.

[25] See Michael Novak, *The Spirit of Democratic Capitalism*, Simon and Schuster, New York, 1982. See also the critique of the neo-conservative Christian defence of capitalism by Charles Davis, *Religion and the Making of Society: Essays in Social Theology*, Cambridge University Press, 1995.

atic theology has, with the aid of extra-Christian philosophical concepts and theories, explicated and developed the content of the basic Gospel truths about the humanity and divinity of Jesus Christ, or about the trinitarian aspects of God, or about the nature of the Christian church community and its structure. So also, it is said, moral theology has, with the aid of extra-Christian ethical concepts and theories (such as the natural law theory, or contemporary 'existentialist' or 'personalist' or feminist ideas) explicated and developed the content of the ethical or moral truths implicit in the Gospels.

However, whatever may be said about the development of dogmatic or systematic theology and its use of extra-Christian or extra-scriptural concepts and theories (such as, for example, the concepts of 'nature', 'person', 'substance', 'authority', 'conscience', 'principle'), the development of moral theology has been very different in that, increasingly, Christian moral theology in its various forms, especially in the Roman Catholic Church, has tended to assume that there is an autonomous Christian ethics on a level with other ethical positions based upon human enquiry.

It is true that dogmatic or systematic theology uses philosophical concepts and theories for its own purposes, but it does not enter into the field of philosophy and claim the right to adjudicate philosophical issues as such. Quite properly, apart from some aberrations, the Christian churches have recognised and respected the autonomy of the realm of 'natural reason' very much as, after some scandals and hesitations, they have largely accepted the autonomy of the natural sciences. Philosophy and science are part of God's created order and they must be valued as such.

However, in the area of moral theology, the Christian churches have themselves entered into the field of what we might call 'natural ethics' and have attempted, in various ways, to formulate a systematic Christian ethics with universalistic pretensions on a wide range of quite specific issues. No doubt, there is a connection between the 'idealistic perfectionism' of the Gospels and the ethics of everyday life, but it is not a deductive connection and it is certainly not clear in most cases how one moves from the one to the other. As was noted before, a number of ethical positions can satisfy the Gospel ideals, and there is no one ethical position which is privileged. It may be that the refusal to use artificial means of contraception is one way for a Christian couple to respond to the Gospels' view of marriage, and one can understand a Christian couple, trying to lead a life of 'perfection', adopting that stance. But it cannot be shown that the Roman Catholic Church's rejection of artificial contraception (while none the less accepting 'natural' forms of contraception) is derivable in a deductive way from the Gospel view of marriage.

The German theologian, Josef Fuchs, has very clearly distinguished the two levels of ethical reflection:

Concrete ethical norms are not divine revelation. They do not become divine revelation by virtue of traditional or official teaching. They are the discoveries of human beings, accepted by Christians . . . I know of no concrete, ethical formulation among those not divinely revealed norms which has been presented by a Church authority as definitive and to be accepted unconditionally. I think that such an authoritative formulation is impossible, since ethical norms, including those of Christians, originate from human evaluation and insight. They are therefore accessible neither solely to authority nor solely to tradition, but to Christians and non-Christians, to bishops, theologians, and laypersons alike.[26]

HISTORICAL ASPECTS

This is, in fact, shown quasi-empirically in the history of the Christian Churches' attempts to formulate a Christian ethic. That complex and confused history demonstrates what a wide range of very different, and often contradictory, derivations about ethical matters have been made in the past from the Gospel values. A brief account of various errors, misapprehensions, flagrant contradictions, wrong turnings, selective interpretations, sudden changes and missed opportunities in the ethical teaching of the Christian Churches shows conclusively what a humanly fallible process the elaboration of that ethical teaching has been. These errors and confusions are a datum that has to be taken into account in any kind of theological analysis of the development of a Christian ethics.

In a recent essay, the American historian, John T. Noonan,

[26] J. Fuchs, *Christian Ethics in a Secular Arena*, Dublin, Gill and Macmillan, 1984, p. 7.

considers a number of examples of radical change in the ethical teaching of the Roman Catholic Church.[27] The first example is the teaching of the medieval church on usury, the practice of taking profit on a loan, which from about 1150 to 1550 was forbidden by two Councils of the church and the ordinary magisterium of the church as being contrary to the natural law and to the law of the church and the law of the Gospel. Those who denied that usury was a serious sin were condemned as heretics.[28] But, from the late sixteenth century onwards, this solemn prohibition was simply abandoned and the morality of taking appropriate interest on loans, now the lynchpin of our commercial world, was accepted by the church without question. As Noonan says:

> The idea that it is against nature for money to breed money, or that it is contrary to church law to deposit in a savings institution with the hope of a profit, or that hoping for profit at all from a loan breaks a command of Christ – all these ideas, once unanimously inculcated with the utmost seriousness by the teaching authority of the Church, are now so obsolete that one invites incredulity by reciting them.[29]

A second example concerns the church's acceptance of the institution of slavery until the late nineteenth century. Early Catholic moral teaching accepted slavery as a given social institution, following the example of St Paul who returned the slave Onesimus to his master[30] and instructed the slaves at Corinth to obey their masters.[31] St Augustine and Pope Gregory the Great also accepted slavery, as did later theologians of the calibre of St Antoninus of Florence and St Thomas Aquinas. At the end of the seventeenth century the great French theologian, Bossuet, roundly declared that to condemn slavery would be, in effect, 'to condemn the Holy Spirit, who by the mouth of St Paul orders slaves to remain in their state'.[32] In the US, Catholic bishops accepted chattel slavery without question until the latter part of the nineteenth century, even though it involved owning another human being and the products of his or her labour, being able to determine where a slave lived, or whether he or she could marry or be educated or punished. In fact, in 1826, the Maryland Province

[27] John T. Noonan, 'Development in Moral Doctrine', *Theological Studies*, 54, 1993, 662–77.
[28] Ibid., 662–3. [29] Ibid. 663. [30] Philemon 10–19. [31] I Corinthians 7, 21.
[32] Noonan, 'Development in Moral Doctrine', p. 666.

of the Society of Jesus owned as slaves 'about 500 African men'.[33] It was held, of course, that slaves should be treated humanely and, where possible, granted freedom, but the institution of slavery remained unquestioned by the church. Certainly, the US Catholic bishops were not in the vanguard of the anti-slavery movement in their country, and the ordinary magisterium of the church ruled in 1866 that to buy and sell slaves was not contrary to the natural law.[34]

From the late nineteenth century, however, the Roman Catholic Church began to condemn slavery and its concomitants as a gross social evil contrary to the dignity of the human person. This reversal of the traditional view culminated in the *Pastoral Constitution on the Church in the Modern World* (*Gaudium et spes*) at the Second Vatican Council.[35]

The third example is that of the church's teaching on the right to freedom of belief of those outside the church. From the time of St Augustine it was part of the teaching of the church that 'heretics' should not be tolerated by the state, and church authorities took an active part in the persecution of those heretics.[36] In 1832, Pope Gregory XVI condemned liberty of conscience as 'the false and absurd, or rather mad principle (*deliramentum* in the Latin text) that we must secure and guarantee to each one liberty of conscience: this is one of the most contagious of errors'. Pius IX, Gregory's successor, repeated the condemnation of liberty of conscience several times, the most severe being in the *Syllabus of Errors* in 1864.[37]

One hundred years after Pius IX's solemn condemnation, in 1965, the Second Vatican Council's *Declaration on Religious Freedom* had this to say:

Man perceives and acknowledges the imperatives of the divine law through the mediation of conscience. In all his activity a man is bound to follow his conscience faithfully, in order that he may come to God, for whom he was created. It follows that he is not to be forced to act in a

---

[33] Ibid. p. 665.   [34] Ibid.

[35] See the *Pastoral Constitution* section 29, in W. M. Abbott ed. *The Documents of Vatican II*, London, Geoffrey Chapman, 1966.

[36] Noonan, 'Development in Moral Doctrine', pp. 667–8.

[37] On the nineteenth-century debate within the Catholic Church on liberty of conscience see Max Charlesworth, 'Newman on Church, State and Conscience', in *Church, State and Conscience*, St Lucia, University of Queensland Press, 1973.

manner contrary to his conscience. Nor, on the other hand, is he to be restrained from acting in accordance with his conscience, especially in matters religious.[38]

The main author of the *Declaration on Religious Freedom*, Fr. John Courtney Murray, has described this remarkable volte-face as a genuine doctrinal 'development',[39] but, while it is indeed a development of the central, but long neglected, idea of conscience, it is also a flat contradiction and rejection of the church's ethical teaching over more than 1600 years.[40]

Apart from Noonan's examples of changes in the ethical teaching of the Roman Catholic Church, one might also mention the church's teaching on the moral status of the human embryo, a central issue in its teaching on abortion, contraception and the new reproductive technologies. The church's present official teaching is that right from the moment of fertilisation the human embryo should be deemed to be, and treated as, a human person, so that destruction of the embryo by abortion, or contraception or experimentation is tantamount to murder.[41] The present position is somewhat ambiguous, in that it is not altogether clear whether it is being said that we do not, and cannot, know, exactly when the embryo becomes 'ensouled' or 'animated' with an intellectual soul, and that it is therefore 'safer' to treat the embryo as though it were a person; or whether it is being said that the embryo is, in fact, a person or 'on the way to becoming a person' (*une personne en devenir*, in the French phrase). However, the latter view seems to be the one favoured by the most recent papal statements.[42]

This position is, however, very different from the traditional Christian position, which appears to have been established by the fourth century and which distinguishes between the early human embryo up to about forty days and the embryo in its later stages

---

[38] *Declaration on Religious Freedom*, section 3, in W. M. Abbott ed. *The Documents of Vatican 11*, London, Geoffrey Chapman, 1966.   [39] Ibid. p. 673.

[40] On the notion of conscience see Timothy Potts, *Conscience in Medieval Philosophy*, Cambridge University Press, 1980. See also Eric D'Arcy, *Conscience and Its Right to Freedom*, London, Sheed and Ward, 1961. Part 1 provides the historical background to Aquinas' discussion of conscience.

[41] See *Instruction on Respect for Human Life in its Origin and on the Dignity of Procreation: Replies to Certain Questions of the Day*, Congregation for the Doctrine of the Faith, Vatican, 1987.

[42] See Michael J. Coughlan, *The Vatican, the Law and the Human Embryo*, London, Macmillan, 1990, for a useful survey.

when it was deemed to be 'formed' and to be 'animated' by an intellectual soul. Before forty days, any attempt to abort the embryo was held to be a sin or moral fault, but it was not the sin of homicide or murder. After forty days, it was deemed to be the killing of a human person or murder. Penances for causing an abortion were accordingly graduated according to the seriousness of the fault as determined by whether it took place before or after forty days of gestation. St Augustine's position is typical:

If what is brought forth (after a miscarriage) is unformed (*informe*) but at this stage some sort of living, shapeless thing (*informiter*), then the law of homicide would not apply, for it could not be said that there was a living soul in that body, since it entirely lacks sense-powers, if it be something not yet formed and therefore not yet endowed with its senses.[43]

This view was held by St Gregory of Nyssa (330–395), St Augustine (354–430), the great legislator Pope Innocent III in the early thirteenth century, and by medieval theologians such as Albertus Magnus and St Thomas Aquinas. Pope Sixtus V, in 1588, went counter to this tradition by espousing a position similar to that now adopted by the Roman Catholic Church, but his teaching was almost immediately reversed by his successor, Gregory XVI, in 1591, and the distinction between the 'unformed' embryo and the 'formed' or 'animate' embryo, and of the differential appropriate moral respect due to both, continued to be observed by canon lawyers and moralists.

This tradition, which attempted to adjust the degree of protection to be given to the developing human embryo and foetus to the stage of embryonic development, was suddenly changed by Pope Pius IX in 1869. Pio Nono threatened excommunication for anyone who caused an abortion of a human embryo or fetus regardless of the stage of its development. Right from the moment of fertlisation the human embryo was deemed to be a person and

---

[43] *Questionum in Hept.*, 1, 11, n. 80. Cited in G. R. Dunstan, 'The Human Embryo in the Western Moral Tradition', in G. R. Dunstan and Mary J. Seller eds., *The Status of the Human Embryo: Perspectives from Moral Tradition*, Oxford University Press, King Edward's Hospital Fund for London, 1988. I rely heavily on Dunstan's excellent essay. See also A. Chollet, 'Animation', in A. Vacant and E. Mangenot eds., *Dictionnaire de théologie catholique*, Paris, Latouzey, 1938, col. 1536ff.; and recent studies, J. Mahoney, *Bioethics and Belief*, London, Sheed and Ward, 1984, and N. M. Ford, *When Did I Begin?* Cambridge University Press, 1988.

was given absolute protection. As noted above, there is a distinction between those, on the one hand, who hold that, since we can never know when an embryo is 'ensouled' or 'animated', and since there is a *possibility* that it is ensouled at the moment of conception, it is morally safer to deem the early embryo (or 'pre-embryo' as the embryo is sometimes called before the crucial phase of implantation) to be a person and to treat it accordingly; and those, on the other hand, who claim that the embryo is *actually* a person.

In any event, Pius IX's teaching was at odds with the ethical tradition that prevailed in the Roman Catholic Church for more than 1500 years. As the Anglican theologian, Gordon Dunstan, puts it:

The claim to absolute protection for the human embryo 'from the beginning' is a novelty in the western, Christian and specifically Roman Catholic moral traditions. It is virtually a creation of the later nineteenth century, a little over a century ago, and that is a novelty indeed as traditions go.[44]

It is commonly said that the traditional view depended on the outmoded biology and embryology of Aristotle and the equally antiquated physiology of Hippocrates and Galen. For Aristotle, of course, the human embryo went through an evolution, the embryo and fetus being first animated with a vegetative soul, then an animal soul and finally an intellective soul proper to a human being. In this account, it was not possible for a human being to begin right from the moment of conception, since the fetus only began to be animated by an intellective soul and thus became distinctively human at about forty days. But, while Aristotle's pseudo-scientific account is no longer tenable, the philosophical point behind it remains valid, namely that the human soul can come into existence only if there is a bodily or material substratum sufficiently complex for the soul to inform. The 'infusion' of the intellective soul into a human being is not a miraculous event which suspends the laws of nature; in Aristotle's theory of matter (*hyle*) and form (*morphe*) the intellective soul is the form which informs or animates the material or biological body and makes it distinctively human. And it can only inform a body which is

---

[44] 'The Human Embryo', p. 40.

complex enough for it. It would be philosophically impossible for Aristotle and his medieval followers for the intellective soul to inform or animate a fertilised human ovum at the moment of conception or a two-celled embryo. As one of Aristotle's great Arabic commentators, Ibn Sina (Avicenna), puts it: 'A soul comes into existence whenever a body suitable for it comes into existence.'[45] In modern scientific terms, a human body suitable to be informed by an intellective soul comes into being only with the beginning of the formation of the foetal nervous system. As the theologian Joseph Donceel says apropos Aristotle's theory of matter and form or hylomorphism:

Hylomorphism cannot admit that the fertilised ovum, the morula, the blastocyst, the early embryo, is animated by the intellectual soul . . . Even God cannot put a human soul into a rock, a plant, or a lower animal, any more than he can make the contour of a circle square.[46]

In this scheme of things we cannot argue that it is possible or probable that the intellective soul might be 'infused' at any moment in the development of the human embryo, and that we must therefore, out of prudence, act as though the early human embryo were ensouled, and treat it accordingly. This position assumes a dualistic (anti-hylomorphic) view of human soul and body in which the human soul is understood as existing independently of the body and as an immaterial entity which can be inserted into the human body at any moment in its development. But that view is a philosophically incoherent one.[47]

A consequence of this is that the point of the traditional doctrine on the status of the human embryo and foetus, that our respect for and treatment of the latter has to be a graduated one, is still valid. Unfortunately, Pio Nono's doctrinal innovation in 1869 has led the Catholic church's ethical teaching on the status of the human embryo into a *cul de sac*.

Finally, a remark must be made about the Christian churches'

---

[45] Ibid., p. 55.

[46] J. Donceel, 'Immediate Animation and Delayed Hominisation', *Theological Studies*, 37, 1976, 127–8.

[47] For further discussion of 'probabilism' in this area see the powerful essay by Carol A. Tauer, 'The Tradition of Probabilism and the Moral Status of the Early Embryo', in Patricia B. Jung and Thomas A. Shannon, eds., *Abortion and Catholicism: The American Debate*, New York, Crossroad, 1988, pp. 54–84.

failure to recognise and reject the historical evil of the inequality of women – in relations between men and women, in the family, in the workplace, in society at large, in the law, and, especially and scandalously, within the Christian church itself. The exclusion of women from the priesthood in the Roman Catholic and Orthodox churches is but one, immensely important, aspect of this connivance between the Christian churches and the prevailing socio-cultural structures.[48]

The remarks above on the various contradictions and failures or inconsistencies of the Roman Catholic Church in the ethical domain are not motivated by any kind of scepticism or malice. Those failures are, after all, simply of the kind that one would expect of a human institution. The Christian church is a human institution, just as the Christian scriptures are in human words and narrative forms. The fact that the church claims that it is the vehicle of a divine message and 'way' and has divine assistance and that the scriptures are 'the word of God', does not alter this fact.

It is worth remembering that Jesus' humanity was real and total, and that he was subject to the restrictions and limitations of his humanity – in the fact that he was born in a particular place and at a particular time, that he was part of a local socio-political culture and of a specific religious context, that he was a man in a culture in which women were devalued, that his teaching was influenced and coloured by the preoccupations of his listeners in a small and remote and atypical part of the world, and so on. Even Jesus' awareness of his divine mission and his identification with 'the Father' was a human awareness and realisation that developed and matured by human questioning and doubt. The fact that Jesus was, as Christians believe, also 'divine' in some sense, does not alter these facts about his humanity.

The Christian church, then, cannot expect that it can, in some miraculous way, escape the limitations and imperfections that attended Jesus' human existence, or that, as a human institution, it will be any less ambiguous than the historical Jesus was. One sometimes gets the impression from some theologians that the task of the Christian church is to remedy the uncertainties and

---

[48] The now classic study is Elisabeth Schüssler Fiorenza, *In Memory of Her: A Feminist Theological Reconstruction of Christian Origins*, New York, Crossroads, 1983.

obscurities and ambiguities of Jesus' own teaching, as though the church can, like some kind of court of appeal, intervene to give a clear and unequivocal and certain interpretation or reading of that teaching. But Jesus did not come to give human beings an infallibly clear and certain message so that everyone knew exactly what they had to believe and do, and neither can the church pretend that it can give an absolutely clear and certain message which would remedy the ambiguities and lacunae of the original message of its Founder. One can therefore regret that the ethical teaching of the church has been deficient and contradictory and misleading in many ways, while not being surprised or scandalised by this fact.

In any case, the point of the above criticisms is not to chide the church for not doing what I have argued it should not do, namely, developing a substantive Christian ethics of its own on issues such as slavery and the equality of women. The point has been, rather, to show that, in historical terms, the church has not been successful in its attempt to develop such an ethic from Gospel values.

NATURAL LAW

A notable feature of Roman Catholic ethical teaching has been its use of the 'natural law'. It is this, in fact, which distinguishes Roman Catholic moral theology from that developed within the Reformed churches, just as 'natural theology' (the attempt to develop strictly philosophical proofs or demonstrations of the existence and basic attributes of God) has been a point of distinction between the two Christian blocs. I am not concerned here with the philosophical validity or invalidity of the natural law theory of ethics, but rather with the way in which the theory (or one version of the theory) has been given an extraordinarily privileged position by being pressed into service by the Roman Catholic Church in its elaboration of what it sees as the Christian ethics.

The term 'natural law' has had a very long history, and has a number of very different meanings.[49] At one level, it refers to the basic and very general principles of morality which are known quasi-intuitively by all human beings when they reflect on moral or

---

[49] For an overview see Josef Fuchs, *Natural Law: A Theological Investigation*, Dublin, Gill, 1965.

ethical issues. Sophocles in his great drama *Antigone* speaks of this basic moral law as being over and above the civil laws of society and as the measure of the justice of the civil law. It was roughly in this sense that St Paul used the term when he spoke of the Gentiles having a basic sense of moral right and wrong.[50]

But there were several different theories about the natural law developed by Greek philosophers. The Stoics, for example, argued that there was a 'natural order' which human beings must attune themselves to if they were to live moral lives. As a recent commentator has put it, for the Stoics:

as we become rational we are supposed to realise that there is a natural, rational order of things of which we are just a part; that we from birth have been constructed in such a way as to help maintain this natural order and to maintain it by means of reason, once we have become rational, and that it is hence the most rational thing for us to do to try as well as we can to maintain this order since, given that eveything is fated, we cannot act against its design anyway.[51]

As we have seen, for the Stoic thinker Seneca, ethics is the pursuit of union with the 'best part of the self' which is identified with the Universal Reason which pervades nature. One becomes 'aware of oneself as a part of Nature, and a portion of Universal Reason'.[52] In this view, then, the ethical life is one that is in harmony with the natural cosmic order of things, and moral evil represents a disruption of this order. It is 'unnatural'.

For Plato, ethics is based not upon cosmic nature but *human* nature. A thing is 'good' when it fulfils its 'function' (*ergon*) well (the eye is in a good state when it fulfils its function of seeing well) and human beings are morally good when they fulfil their function (as rational beings with bodily instincts and emotions needing to be controlled) well. Moral goodness consists in the rational and non-rational 'parts of the soul' being in harmony, and moral evil consists in them being out of order.[53] Similarly, Aristotle thinks that human beings have certain ends which are directed towards the

[50] Romans 2. 12–16.
[51] Michael Frede, 'The Affections of the Soul', in M. Schofield and G. Striker eds., *The Norms of Nature: Studies in Hellenistic Ethics*, Cambridge University Press, 1986, p. 109.
[52] P. Hadot, *Philosophy as a Way of Life*, p. 211.
[53] Plato, *The Republic*, Harmondsworth, Penguin, 1983, pp. 434–45.

supreme end of happiness (*eudaimonia*), the most complete and flourishing human state. In this sense ethics is founded upon human nature. But human nature for Aristotle is not a fixed and immutable structure with a determined set of teleological tendencies (like plants or animals); the intellectual 'soul' informs the physical body with its instinctual and emotional drives and tendencies, which are, as it were, its 'matter' (*hyle*). It is what human beings *do* with the latter, and the way we exploit and develop their potentialities and give them expressive meaning, that humanises them. We will not discover anything about how we should act sexually by inspecting the physical or biological sexual apparatus and the sexual instincts; it is only when we *use* those biological means and instincts to express our love for another or to form a family community that we are acting in a human and ethical way. We can (as Aristotle does in the *Nicomachean Ethics*) specify certain ways of acting as good, and we can sketch a portrait, so to speak, of the good human person with all the appropriate character traits or 'virtues' (*aretai*) – justice, temperance, courage, friendship, truthfulness. But we cannot formulate ethical commandments or 'principles' save of the most general kind: one should strive to be courageous; one should be just etc. More specific rules or maxims of ethical practice (one should always pay one's debts etc.) can never be 'absolute' and unchangeable or 'exceptionless'. As Aristotle says in the *Nichomachean Ethics*:

matters of practice and questions of what is advantageous never stand fixed any more than do matters of health. For such cases do not fall under any science (*techne*) or precept, but the agents themselves must in each case look to what suits the occasion, as is also the case in medicine and navigation.[54]

The version of the natural law theory favoured by Roman Catholic moral theologians is that found in St Thomas Aquinas' Treatise on Law in the *Summa Theologiae*.[55] Aquinas' Treatise on Law is a summary account of the various kinds of law, and is very much influenced by the system of Roman Law with which he was familiar. It is, in a sense, an essay in jurisprudence rather than an essay in ethics proper, and the strictly ethical part, if one may so put

[54] 1104 a3–10.   [55] 1a 2ae, questions 90–114.

it, on the 'natural law' is subordinated to this larger plan. The primary precepts of the natural law are proposed as 'laws' or general commands and they are said to be 'self-evident' and to be 'unchangeable',[56] though exceptions are admitted for certain actions commanded or allowed by God in the Old Testament (the command to Abraham to kill his son; the toleration of polygamy with regard to the early Israelites etc.) But derivations from the primary precepts (for example, that private ownership of property is a good social institution) are not self-evident, nor are they unchangeable. It is the function of the civil law to specify ways and means of putting the very general moral principles of the natural law into practice, and there may be very different ways and means of doing this depending on the circumstances.

If one were confined to the Treatise on Law, it would be difficult to discern what St Thomas Aquinas' view of ethics really was. But it is clear that Aquinas did not ever see his sketchy remarks about the natural law in the Treatise as constituting his entire ethical theory. That theory is, in fact, contained in the Treatise on Human Acts in the *Summa Theologiae*,[57] where Aquinas closely follows Aristotle's *Nicomachean Ethics*. Here there is no mention of the 'natural law', any more than there is in Aristotle, and there is an emphasis not on ethical 'principles' or 'precepts', but on 'virtues' or the character dispositions that the good human being should have. There is also a focus on the detailed working out of ethical rules in particular circumstances, and of the need for 'prudence', which is Aquinas' version of Aristotle's 'practical wisdom' (*phronesis*).

In this area we cannot speak of absolute and unchangeable commandments about 'intrinsically' good or evil acts, since an act is characterisable as 'murder', or 'truthfulness' or 'courage' only in a context or set of circumstances. In a particular set of circumstances, this act, which involves directly and intentionally taking the life of this person who is not threatening my life and who is innocent of any wrongdoing, can be described or characterised as 'murder'. In another set of circumstances, where the other is threatening my

---

[56] 1a 2ae, 94, 2 and 5.

[57] Daniel Mark Nelson *The Priority of Prudence: Virtue and Natural Law in Thomas Aquinas and the Implications for Modern Ethics*, University Park, Pa., Penn State University Press, 1992, pp. 121–2.

life, exactly the same act can be described as 'justifiable homicide'.
As a recent study of Aquinas' ethical theory argues:

Nature provides only the most general sort of guidance in the sense that
natural inclinations provide the very wide boundaries within which
prudential reason operates. In other words, according to Thomas'
account of our inclinations, practical reason under the direction of
prudence is concerned with physical, social, intellectual, and spiritual
goods. We do not naturally know, however, how many of those goods are
rightly (which is to say, reasonably and virtuously) to be obtained, except
in the sense that it is natural for rational creatures to reason about such
matters. We do not have natural knowledge of the moral species of acts.
The moral specification of acts is a prudential judgment of practical
reason.[58]

The ethical teaching of the Roman Catholic Church has therefore
been developed in a very curious way. It has given a privileged
status to the idea of 'natural law' as it presented in Aquinas'
Treatise on Law in the *Summa Theologiae*, and it has neglected the
very different Aristotelian theory of ethics elaborated by Aquinas in
the Treatise on Human Acts. But, even in its interpretation of the
Treatise on Law, it has misread Aquinas' position, in that it has
ascribed an absolute and unchanging character to secondary or
derivative precepts, even though, for Aquinas, that character
applies only to the very general and quasi-intuitive primary
precepts of the natural law. To use a contemporary example, the
prohibition against *in vitro* fertilisation cannot, on Aquinas' prem-
isses, be an 'absolute' one, since it is clearly a secondary and
derivative matter concerned with prudential decisions about the
ways and means of effecting virtuous sexual and marital relationships.

What appears to be the case is that the teaching authority of the
Roman Catholic Church has been anxious to emphasise the
absolute and unchanging and 'exceptionless' character of the
moral principles or precepts it wished to assert, and, with these
requirements in mind, so to speak, it has selectively interpreted the
natural law tradition and developed a new and revised version.
This, in turn, has had a number of untoward consequences in that
it is difficult to defend this version philosophically, and also in that

[58] Ibid.

it has led to the development of a number of dubious ethical doctrines, for example, about 'intrinsically evil' acts, and also about acts that have a 'double effect'.[59]

ETHICAL TRUTHS AS TRUTHS OF SALVATION

In the very first article of the *Summa Theologiae*,[60] Aquinas makes the point that, although theoretically all human beings can know what the basic ethical precepts are, in practice human failings often prevent this. Christian revelation, however, reminds people of these basic precepts, though the latter are not part of revelation proper, but belong to the order of natural reason. Practically speaking, then, the church has a remedial function with regard to the natural law. This doctrine is a surprising one, since the natural law is supposed to be known by human enquiry, just as philosophical truths are known by natural reason without any help from Christian revelation, and just as, of course, scientific truths are known without aid from revelation. If the church reminds people of certain matters belonging to the natural law, that 'reminder' has to be validated in terms of natural reason and human enquiry. One cannot understand or validate the dictates of the natural law by appealing to faith! Again, as we have seen, in the past the Church has, on a number of occasions (usury, slavery etc.), made serious mistakes about the content of the natural law, so that the teaching authority of the church cannot plausibly claim to be the final arbiter of the natural law.

However, the Roman Catholic Church has extended this doctrine even further by arguing that, since the Church is concerned with human salvation, and since salvation requires that human beings follow the precepts of the natural law, the church therefore, as the divinely appointed guide to salvation, has the right to stand in judgment upon and to interpret the natural law. In other words, ethical truths established by human enquiry are also 'truths of salvation' subject to the teaching authority of the church.

---

[59] See John Dedek, 'Intrinsically Evil Acts: the Emergence of a Doctrine', *Recherches de théologie ancienne et médiévale*, 50, 1983, 191–226, and Josef Fuchs, *Christian Ethics in a Secular Arena*, Washington, Georgetown University Press, 1984, p. 89.

[60] 1a, question 1, art. I.

The germ of this position can be found in Aquinas,[61] but it has been elaborated by some modern theologians, who have held, for instance, that the church's ethical teaching on sexual matters contained in the encyclical *Humanae Vitae* is a 'truth of salvation that obliges on pain of sin'.[62]

A formal statement of the doctrine that the church has the right to interpret the natural law was made in 1968 by Pope Paul VI in the encylical *Humanae Vitae* on artificial contraception:

No member of the faithful could possibly deny that the Church is competent in her magisterium to interpret the natural moral law. It is in fact indisputable . . . that Jesus Christ, when he communicated his divine power to Peter and the other apostles and sent them out to teach all nations his commandments, constituted them as the authentic guardians and interpreters of the whole moral law, not only, that is, of the law of the gospel but also of the natural law, the reason being that the natural law declares the will of God, and its faithful observance is necessary for men's eternal salvation.[63]

This is an extraordinary doctrine since, prima facie, it seems to confuse the realms of faith and understanding, or the realms of religious revelation and human ethical enquiry. In traditional Catholic thinking, matters of revelation are by definition beyond the scope of human enquiry, and they are ultimately believed by faith. Conversely, matters of science and philosophy and ethics are the result of human enquiry, and they are not subject to religious faith. Since they can be known by reason, it is otiose to say that they can be believed by faith. It is difficult, indeed, to understand how ethical norms could be accepted by faith, since, if a person is to act ethically, they have in some way to appreciate and accept the reasons that support and justify a given norm. If someone were to say that they respected the lives of other human beings solely because they accepted the teaching of the church on this matter, and with no regard at all to the reasons that might be given for respecting the lives of others, we would be inclined to say that that person was not acting as an autonomous and conscientious ethical agent. In making authentic ethical decisions, one cannot conscien-

---

[61] II, II, 148, 4 ad 1.
[62] See on this Josef Fuchs, 'Moral Truths – Truths of Salvation', in *Christian Ethics in a Secular Arena*, pp. 48–67.   [63] St Paul Editions, 1968, section 4.

tiously abandon the use of one's own conscience and simply follow the advice of others, no matter how 'divinely guided' the latter might claim to be. In any case, the church, in its ethical statements on matters like abortion, embryo experimentation, euthanasia, *in vitro* fertilisation etc., argues in ordinary philosophical terms and justifies its position in those terms. One can hardly say that, even if its philosophical arguments are deficient or incoherent, its statements are nevertheless 'truths of salvation' and must be accepted by faith.

Again, whatever may be the position of those Christians who accept the teaching authority of the Roman Catholic Church, it is difficult to see how other Christians, and especially those who do not believe in the Christian revelation at all, might be expected to accept the Roman Catholic Church's interpretation of the natural law. Since it can never be a moral fault not to believe in a particular religious revelation, save perhaps in the case where one first decides that a revelation is true and then refuses to make a commitment to it, there cannot be any obligation on a non-believer to accept the ethical prescriptions of the Catholic 'magisterium'.

In a sense, of course, Christian revelation makes a number of philosophical and ethical presuppositions of a very general kind, for example, that the notion of a personal and providential God is an intelligible one and that human beings are capable of making a response to this God and of engaging in free and autonomous ethical acts. Certain philosophical positions are thereby excluded (for example, the various forms of philosophical atheism and materialism), but the Church does not, and cannot, positively endorse or give a privileged status to any one philosophical position (although in the Thomist revival in the late nineteenth and early twentieth centuries some over-enthusiastic Thomists appeared to argue that Aquinas' 'five ways' of philosophical proof of the existence of God must be taken as matters of faith).

In the same way, while the church makes ethical presuppositions that exclude certain ethical positions (for example, forms of ethical subjectivism and relativism and sociobiological determinism) it does not, and cannot positively favour and endorse any one ethical position. Members of the church, as human beings, will have to understand and follow the basic ethical precepts for themselves through their own enquiry and insight. As was noted above: 'Concrete ethical norms are not divine revelation. They do not become divine revelation by virtue of traditional or official teaching. They are the discoveries of human beings, accepted by Christians.'[64] Just as, according to the old scholastic maxim, 'grace does not do away with nature but perfects it', so the ethical teaching of the church concerned with the order of grace and 'perfection' does not do away with the need for the ethics of human enquiry but complements it and 'perfects' it.

A final remark: it is worthwhile emphasising that in the above discussion it is not being implied that the Christian churches should opt out of the ethical and socio-ethical spheres and, as some politicians sometimes suggest, confine themselves to the vestry. Christians, animated by the values and spirit of the Gospels, ought to be intensely concerned with ethical issues that arise in personal matters such as sexuality and reproduction, genetic intervention, family relationships, and in such social matters as peace and war, the distribution of wealth, obligations to the poor and needy, the equality of women, the natural environment, population growth and so on. But, when they do engage with such issues, they have to rely on the same kind of human enquiry that everyone uses, and they have to obey the same canons of reasoning and argue their case in the same way that everyone – Christians and non-Christians and anti-Christians alike – must do. Their positions are only as good as the reasons and arguments they support them with. They cannot pretend that their ideas have some kind of revelationary or *de fide* status and divine support.

Again, as we have seen, while certain ethical positions are consonant with the Gospel values, and while others are excluded as being in opposition to those values, a number of diverse positions can satisfy the requirements of the Gospel, and no one position can claim to have a privileged status as the sole legitimate Christian position. In other words, the position of Christianity with regard to the ethical and social orders is of necessity a pluralistic one. There is an old saying that the saints are admirable, but not imitable, and the same is true of the ethical positions of individual Christians.

[64] Fuchs, *Christian Ethics in a Secular Arena*, p. 7.

CONCLUSION

If what has been said here has any substance, then the idea that there is a distinct Christian ethic which, at least in principle, has universal application, needs to be radically rethought. The Roman Catholic Church has developed this idea in the most systematic and complete way, but other Christian churches have also, in different modes, held that their task was to present a distinctively Christian body of ethical truths on a level with, and in competition with, what I have called the ethics of human enquiry. The ethical positions on abortion and euthanasia and homosexuality of fundamentalist evangelical churches in the US are but one example of this. These Christians assume that the ethics of the Bible (as they interpret it) applies not just to Christian believers, but to everyone, Christian and non-Christians alike, and they call upon the state to legislate their ethical position for all members of their society. In other words, they argue that the ethics of their particular religious revelation (as they interpret it) should become universally applicable for all members of society whether or not they are believers in that revelation.

Apart from the dangerous implications of this position for any liberal society characterised by ethical pluralism,[65] it distorts the mission of the Christian churches and distracts them from what ought to be their main task in promoting the way of Christian perfection. Christian are now known more by their attitudes on issues such as abortion, euthanasia, artificial contraception and so on, than they are by their following of the precepts of the Sermon on the Mount. The riches of the long and diverse tradition of Christian 'mysticism' – the experiential following out of the way of perfection or the spiritual life – are hardly mentioned.

As has been said already, if there is no place for a Christian ethic of the kind we have been discussing, the whole discipline of moral theology must be rethought. Moral theology, especially in the Roman Catholic Church, has been an unfortunate construction or invention, and it will not be easy to deconstruct it and centre it upon the modalities of the Christian life of perfection. That,

[65] See Max Charlesworth, *Bioethics in a Liberal Society*, Cambridge University Press, 1994.

however, will have liberating effects on moral theologians in that it will disencumber them from a lot of baggage that they should really have no direct concern with.

Finally, the point needs to be reiterated that this does not have any kind of quietistic implications, as though the Christian moral theologian should retire altogether from ethical and social activism. A Christian, living the life of Christian perfection, will be sensitive to, and concerned with, all the issues that arise in God's world. But he or she will have to deal with those issues in much the same way as other people do, by using the resources of human enquiry. (I have already suggested that this is, in fact, what Christians, and the Christian churches, actually do.) As was said before, philosophy and science are part of God's created order, and they have their own autonomous value. The same is true of that part of philosophy I have called the ethics of human enquiry. The fact that Christian revelation, or any other revelation, discloses an order of grace, a 'way of perfection', does not mean that we have to deny the value of the order of creation including the ethics of human reflection. It has to be seen rather as something to be complemented or raised to a higher power or 'perfected'.

Conclusion

One might imagine that vast and mysterious (yet familiar) territory we call 'religion' as a kind of Amazonian jungle: some parts dense and impenetrable, other areas with great rivers flowing serenely through them, unexpected clearings where minutely small human settlements have created astonishingly original ways of life for themselves, other settlements whose inhabitants seem to live oppressed and brutish and fearful existences, vistas of marvellous beauty and swamps of foreboding darkness devoid of sunlight and life. The jungle is so vast and so various that we know it can never be fully explored or mapped. The more we explore parts of it, the more we are confronted by radical surprises of all kinds and the more we have to readjust our anticipations and redraw our crude maps.

The four essays that make up the main part of this book are no more than tentative and partial forays into the Amazonian jungle of religion, and, it goes without saying, they make no claim to provide a map of the whole terrain. No doubt, some lessons can be learned from those limited forays – that no religion can really claim to be the exclusively 'true' religion (though it may claim to be a paradigmatic form of religion); that the diversity of revelations is not an unfortunate accident due to human ignorance or sinfulness but something to be wholly expected; that the so-called 'primal' religions (like those of Aboriginal Australia) deserve to be taken as seriously as the so-called 'world religions'; that the same is true of the myriad, sometimes eccentric and bizarre (as they appear to us), religious sects; that there is a dialectical tension in all religions between the universal and local elements or between the original revelation and the traditions that enable that revelation to be lived by human beings, and that an exaggeration of one or the other can result in religious pathology; that there is a sense in which religions, while providing an ethical perspective, cannot provide a complete way of life or ethic but must recognise the place of an ethic based on human enquiry and reflection.

However, these findings do not enable us to define the essence of religion, or the 'divine' or the 'numinous', in the confident style of the great nineteenth- and twentieth-century scholars of comparative religion. Nor, of course, do they provide criteria which would enable us to adjudicate between specific religions. As I have said, my method precludes any such attempts: instead, the essays are a kind of celebration of the differences between religious systems rather than an attempt to coerce them into some kind of procrustean framework.

That method, if it can be dignified as such, follows from the thesis that religion is what we humans make of that gratuitous event we call a religious revelation. What we take to be a revelation of 'the divine' (to use the convenient Greek term) has to be received by us and interpreted and 'localised', just as, in the ethical realm, universal values have to be incarnated in particular situations. That whole process requires human invention, or creation, or construction, or making, which is analogous to the invention or making of human languages, and which involves an element of gratuitousness on our part. There is, so to speak, no one necessary or 'natural' way to respond, since the response must be spontaneous and creative. As I have noted, this is a common-sense thesis which does not rest on any high theory; however, it is a thesis whose radical implications are often ignored. For example, what is loosely called 'fundamentalism' is, in fact, an attempt to deny any kind of human invention in religion.

Because the human response to revelation is creative and gratuitous and unpredictable, the only way it can be 'investigated' is through particular examples or cases of invention. (Despite some of its oddities, William James' great work, *The Varieties of Religious Experience*, now almost one hundred years old, clearly recognised this fact.) In this kind of enquiry, philosophy (in a broad sense) plays a large part. No doubt, to the philosophical purist it is not 'pure' philosophy, but many issues continually come up that can only be clarified by philosophical analysis and what I would call philosophical imagination (seeing relevant analogies, for example). One might mention here issues about the inescapability of interpretation and whether this leads to relativism; religious 'experience' and the interpretation of that experience; the notion of 'truth' in religious systems and whether such systems are 'incommensurable' in much the same way as it has been claimed scientific systems are; universal truths and local knowledge; the conditions of possibility of ethics and whether a universal ethical commitment can be based upon a particular religious commitment. It seems to me that a good deal of scholarly discussion of religions suffers from the lack of philosophical awareness and *nous* of this kind.

MEISTER ECKHART AND SISTER KATREI

Apart from my four cases or examples of religious invention, there are, of course, many others that lend themselves to fruitful analysis of the kind I advocate. Religious experience or mystical experience is a field where one can often see the process of creative invention at work in a vivid way. In my first essay, I mentioned the extraordinary late twelfth- and early thirteenth-century Rhineland mystic (mystical philosopher would be a better description) Meister Eckhart. There I was mainly interested in showing that the religious experience Eckhart described could not be abstracted from the interpretive framework which gave it meaning. But it is also of the greatest interest to see how, while remaining entirely within the Christian tradition, Eckhart creates a highly original account of the interchange and negotiation between the human and the divine in the mystical encounter.

Eckhart had studied at the University of Paris in 1293–4 and later taught in the Faculty of Arts there in 1302–3 and 1311–13. As a member of the Dominican order, Eckhart had been inducted into the form of Christianised (and Neoplatonised) Aristotelianism elaborated by his fellow Dominicans Albertus Magnus and Thomas Aquinas earlier in the thirteenth century. Eckhart was sent back to Germany in 1313 to provide spiritual direction to the large and vigorous movement of religious women in convents, and the lay women called beguines, who, as it has been said, 'transformed the Rhine valley into a veritable laboratory of the religious life'.[1] The beguines, who had some links with the radical spiritual movement of the 'Free Spirit', did not follow a formal religious rule and did not seek authorisation from their bishops or the pope.[2] Consequently they alarmed the Church authorities and suffered several official condemnations.[3]

One gets some impression of their fervent and heady ideas from the celebrated dialogue written by one of Eckhart's beguines, Sister Katrei or Catherine. In the dialogue, Katrei announces to her confessor, 'Father rejoice with me, I have become God.' Her confessor calmly replies: 'If you remain God I will rejoice with you.' Katrei later sinks into an ecstatic swoon which lasts for three days. Her friends think that she is dead and are about to bury her, but she recovers consciousness and her confessor asks her: 'Reveal your experience to me.' 'God knows that I cannot', Katrei replies, 'I cannot tell anyone what I have experienced.' The confessor persists: 'Now do you have everything you want?' 'Yes', says Katrei, 'I am granted everlasting bliss. I have attained by grace what Christ is by nature.' Later in the dialogue she says: 'I am established in the pure Godhead in which there was never form nor image.'[4]

Eckhart provided his enthusiastic charges with, so to speak, a theory of the spiritual life which enabled them to make sense of their experience. That theory was, in effect, a novel reinterpretation of his near contemporary (and fellow Dominican) Albert the Great's transformation of Aristotle's idea, that happiness consisted

---

[1] Alain de Libera, *Penser au moyen âge*, Paris, Editions du Seuil, 1991, p. 306.

[2] See Robert E. Lerner, *The Heresy of the Free Spirit in the Later Middle Ages*, Berkeley, University of California Press, 1972.

[3] On the beguines see the introduction to F. Bowie ed., *Beguine Spirituality: An Anthology*, London, SPCK, 1989; P. Dronke, *Women Writers of the Middle Ages: A Critical Study of Texts from Perpetua to Marguerite Porete*, Cambridge University Press, 1984; Elizabeth Petroff, *Medieval Women's Visionary Literature*, New York, Oxford University Press, 1986. See chapter 4 on the beguine movement.

[4] Katrei's dialogue has been translated as 'This is About the Confessor's Daughter', in Bernard McGinn ed., *Meister Eckhart: Teacher and Preacher*, New York, Paulist Press, 1986, Appendix 1, see pp. 258–9, 361. For a discussion of Katrei's dialogue see pp. 10–14. See also de Libera, *Penser*, p. 311, and de Libera, *Introduction à la mystique rhénane*, Paris, OEIL, 1984.

in philosophical contemplation, into an ascetical doctrine that this contemplation required progressive detachment from the world of the senses. Albert himself had been influenced in this by the great Islamic Aristotelian, Ibn Sina (Avicenna), who had identified Aristotle's life of philosophical contemplation with the prophetic life. Eckhart, in turn, reformulated this idea in his doctrine of radical detachment (*abegescheidenheit*) which leads to the indwelling of God in the soul. With Eckhart, then, Aristotle's ideas about the philosophical life had been transformed into a doctrine about the mystical life for the religious women and beguines of the Rhineland. As has been said:

Due to Eckhart, and through the links established between the Dominicans and certain religious communities of Alsace and the Rhineland [this doctrine] had, in a sense, gained a new public, a non-university public, a partially lay public and, above all, a feminine public – religious women and beguines.[5]

Those women, in turn, provided him with a rich store of experiential data, and it is fascinating to see how the philosopher from the University of Paris and the women who made up the Rhineland movement (it has been estimated that there were more than a thousand women involved) mutually fabricated a highly original (and 'orthodox', despite Eckhart's later condemnation in 1329) account of the 'way of perfection'. Eckhart and other Dominican spiritual directors in the Rhineland developed a special style of sermons which, it has been said, was 'the product of a fusion of Dominican theological training and the raw mystical experience of the women'. They 'appropriate and extend the organic spirituality of the women into the conceptual sphere'.[6] The mystical experience of the women was hardly 'raw', since it occurred in a Christian context and was interpreted in Christian terms, but it certainly needed to be put within a larger theoretical framework, and that was provided by Eckhart and his Dominican confrères.

---

[5] Alain de Libera, *La philosophie médiévale*, Paris, Presses Universitaires de France, 1993, p. 404. See especially the remarkable study of Albert the Great's influence on Eckhart, pp. 398–404.

[6] Oliver Davies, *Meister Eckhart: Mystical Theologian*, London, SPCK, 1991, p. 77. Davies is citing the work of the German scholar Grundmann. See Part I, section 3, 'Meister Eckhart and the Religious Women of his Age', in Davies' admirable study.

SECTS

A very different example of religious invention is provided by the seventeenth-century English antinomian sects I have mentioned in my third essay. In his book on the background to William Blake, the historian E. P. Thompson recounts the moving story of the religious sect of Muggletonians ('a peculiar people' as they called themselves).[7] The sect was founded by 'the prophets' Ludowick Muggleton and his cousin John Reeve in 1652. Reeve and Muggleton saw themselves as 'Messengers of a Third Commission' from God which was to usher in a New Age. The first commission was that of the Old Testament and the Law; the second was that of the New Testament and the Gospel of Jesus Christ; and the third was that of the Spirit.[8] The new religion had little formal organisation, and appealed mainly to artisans and tradespeople. Though at any one time the members in the whole of England barely exceeded 500, the Muggletonians lasted for some 300 years (the last member dying in 1980). The sect was very disputatious and carried on a vigorous paper war about general theological issues, not only with the established church, but also with other sectarian groups, especially the Quakers. Although they were very much against 'learned divines', they engaged in a good deal of high flown theological speculation and polemic of their own. They were, as Thompson nicely observes, 'highly intellectual disciples of an anti-intellectual doctrine'.[9]

It is, of course, tempting for us to see religious sects of this kind as eccentric and rather bizarre developments which usually have a transient life-span and are of interest only to the historian or sociologist or anthropologist. However, it is worth remembering that sectarian religions are, in a sense, much more in the mainstream of religion than the so-called world-religions are. If we

---

[7] E. P. Thompson, *Witness Against the Beast: William Blake and the Moral Law*, Cambridge University Press, 1993.   [8] Ibid., p. 70.

[9] Ibid. p. 90. For an exotic example of sectarian millenarianism see Jonathan Spence's vivid account of the Taiping movement in early nineteenth-century China. See Jonathan Spence, *God's Chinese Son: The Taiping Heavenly Kingdom of Hong Xiuquan*, London, Harper Collins, 1996. The founder of the movement, Hong Xiuquan, drew upon traditional Taoist and Buddhist ideas, Christian themes introduced into China by American Baptist missionaries and English Protestant evangelicals, and his own religious experiences in the 1840s that he was the younger Son of God, Jesus being the elder Son.

count the thousands of religions of small primal peoples, like the Australian Aborigines, as sects, as well as the sectarian groups of the ancient world, the medieval world and later centuries like the fourteenth or seventeenth centuries in Europe, and if we remember the thousands of sects in the Indian and Asian cultures, it is the great world-religions that appear eccentric.[10]

It is worth remembering also that most of the major world-religions – for example, Buddhism, Christianity, Islam – began their careers as sectarian offshoots of another religion. Civilised Romans and Greeks in the first and second centuries of the Christian era saw the new sect of Christianity in very much the same condescending and dismissive way as we now see the Muggletonians.[11] In any case, Thompson challenges this kind of dismissal of the Muggletonians.

I will suggest [he says], that – a few peripheral doctrines apart – Muggletonian beliefs were logical, powerful in their symbolic operations and have only been held to be 'ridiculous' because the Muggletonians were losers and because their faith was professed by 'poor enthusiasts' and not by scholars, bishops or successful evangelists.[12]

However, while one can be sympathetic to Thompson's view here – history, as they say, is always written by the victors – the fact that the Muggletonians were finally 'losers' does show that their religious movement was not able to act as an expressive religious tradition which would allow creative development or reinvention. As Thompson himself notes:

By the mid-eighteenth century we can see that they were a recondite sect, whose beliefs appeared to outsiders as impenetrable and esoteric (if not obscene and blasphemous), whose closet and chest of manuscripts enclosed the sleeping energies of a half-forgotten spiritual and political vocabulary.[13]

---

[10] A US sociological survey has shown that in the decade between 1965 and 1975 three hundred new religious movements appeared in the Bay Area of San Francisco, though the same survey shows that these movements attract a relatively small percentage of the population. See Robert Wuthnow, *The Consciousness Reformation*, Berkeley, University of California Press, 1976, pp. 30–42.

[11] See, for example, Porphyry, *On the Life of Plotinus and His Work*, 16, on Christan 'sectaries' who 'fooled many, themselves fooled in turn'. In *Plotinus. The Enneads*, ed. John Dillon, London, Penguin Classics, 1991, p. cxiv.   [12] *Witness Against the Beast*, p. 79.

[13] Ibid. p. 90.

The inventive impulse had petered out.

One might draw an analogy here with movements or traditions in art – for example, the Pre-Raphaelite movement in mid nineteenth-century England, or the Russian Suprematist movement in the 1920s – which had their own limited value, but did not have the inner resources to become an expressive vehicle for painting on a larger scale. This is a pragmatic (in the Jamesian sense) criterion of the value of artistic and religious movements, and it is difficult to apply, but it clearly has some validity. Again, as I have noted in the third essay, there is always a dialectical relationship between the universal and local elements in religious traditions, and the sectarian phenomenon can be seen as being due to an imbalance in that relationship.

INVENTING VIRGINITY

As a final example of a religious development which displays the role of invention, it is worth remarking the appearance in early Christianity of the ideal of consecrated sexual abstinence or virginity. In a masterly work, the historian, Peter Brown, has shown how the early Christian ideal of virginity – very different from Greek and Roman ideas of ritual virginity – was gradually evolved as a style of Christian life between the time of St Paul and the death of St Augustine in AD 430.[14] That ideal was out of tune with the traditional Judaism from which the first Christians came, and equally at odds with Roman views about the social importance of marriage. It was also not unequivocally supported by Jesus' teaching (the fact that Jesus was himself unmarried was not seen by his earlier followers as an example to be followed), nor even by St Paul in his ambiguous instructions to the Corinthians on sexual abstinence.[15]

The early Christians were then faced with a number of possibilities: they could have, for instance, remained faithful to the Jewish view of the centrality of the married state, or, in the light of the common belief in the imminent advent of Jesus' Kingdom, they

---

[14] Peter Brown, *The Body and Society: Men, Women and Sexual Renunciation in Early Christianity*, London, Faber, 1989.

[15] I Corinthians 7. 12–37, On St Paul see Brown, *The Body and Society*, pp. 49–57.

could have seen virginity as the appropriate state for the Christian. In a sense, there was nothing necessitating them to take the course they did take, namely seeing virginity as an important part of the way of perfection for those who chose the monastic life.

The ideal of consecrated virginity had to be balanced against Jesus' endorsement of permanent and monogamous marriage, and a complex and uneasy theory about the Christian 'states of life' was constructed. Those who embraced virginity and the other sacrificial modalities of the monastic life (poverty, obedience, stability) were thought to be in a higher state of life in that they were more explicitly dedicated to God and less open to the temptations and diversions of ordinary married and family life. On the other hand, those Christians who were married and had families (the majority of the early Christian communities) were totally capable of leading Christian lives. However, with regard to this latter, it is true to say that the Christian churches have never developed a theological view of the married state as a way of Christian life. As a Catholic theologian has said: 'Historically, the specifically Roman Catholic view comes more from canon law and natural law than from the Bible.'[16]

RELIGIOUS PATHOLOGY

I have mentioned the notion of religious pathology several times, and this raises the general question as to what criteria we appeal to when we judge a movement as not being an authentic religion but mere religiosity, or a pseudo-religion, or rank superstition? Certainly, as I have noted, if in a certain sense we invent religions, we can invent them badly. As we have seen in our four case studies, there is (if we needed reminding) such a thing as religious pathology.

We have already noted some prima facie criteria such as the pragmatic test. However, I wish to concentrate here on a fundamental criterion which derives from the thesis that religious traditions are human inventions in the sense that any revelation of the divine has to be received by human beings and interpreted and

---

[16] Lisa Sowle Cahill, 'Marriage', in *Commentary on the Catechism of the Catholic Church*, p. 328.

mediated by them so that they can live it. The denial of this, or the attempted denial, since it can never be successful, implies that there is no place for human reception and interpretation and mediation, and pretends that a revelation imposes itself upon us with some kind of coercive necessity which allows no scope for creative response. The divine overwhelms us (as St Paul was overwhelmed on the road to Damascus) and our only response is to bow before it and submit to it. We have no choice. Any other response is human hubris, where the finite human being attempts to stand in judgment on the infinite God and to mediate that's God's revelation, or to pit his or her will as a creature against the all-powerful will of the creator.

That denial of the human mediation of any revelation is, so I argue, the basis of most forms of religious pathology. As I remarked before, the denial can never be successful, since we cannot really escape the fact that we must receive and interpret and mediate whatever message is given to us by God. Just as in the ethical sphere I must choose and decide for myself what I am about to do, otherwise the act is not *mine* and I am not responsible for it and it has no moral value for me (this is the essence of the doctrine of conscience), so also in the religious sphere I must appropriate the revelation of the divine or God's message for myself. I can never refuse that responsibility any more than I can refuse to choose and decide for myself, since I cannot conscientiously decide not to decide for myself. If religious commitment or faith is an *act*, my act, then my creative response to a revelation cannot be denied without falling into paradox, as though God's grace could coerce me to believe against my will.

We can, of course, attempt to evade our responsibility here and pretend that we have been overwhelmed by God (in conversion experiences, by miracles, by 'grace' and so on), but these attempts are analogous to what Sartre calls 'bad faith' (*mauvaise foi*), the paradoxical attempt to evade the fact that we are free and responsible for ourselves and for our religious commitments.[17]

---

[17] Jean-Paul Sartre, *Being and Nothingness*, trans. Hazel E. Barnes, New York, Washington Square Press, 1966.

THE ROOT OF FUNDAMENTALISM

Scriptural fundamentalism is the position that the words of scripture, being the words of God, are immediately meaningful just as they are and do not need human interpretation or mediation. This is, of course, an ideal description, and no one actually practices this kind of fundamentalism. There is, in fact, a spectrum of fundamentalist stances, some very sophisticated and some vulgar, but what is common to them all is the attempt to deny what I have called the human invention involved in our approach to a scriptural revelation.[18] Apart from scriptural fundamentalism, there is what might be called institutional fundamentalism. Some Christian churches recognise that the scriptures must be interpreted, but they then claim that the church authorities – whether they be church councils, or the pope or some other agency – have the sole power to provide a final and definitive interpretation of the scriptures, as well as of questions of doctrine and moral practice. Those authoritative interpretations, it is claimed, do not themselves need interpretation or human mediation. Since the church authorities are the final arbiters they cannot themselves be subject to any other arbiter, otherwise we would end in an infinite regress. One might see an analogy here with Thomas Hobbes' famous theory of sovereignty in his great work *Leviathan*. For Hobbes, a group of people is a society only if there is a sovereign power who can make absolute and final arbitrations between the members of society who have consented (by a 'social contract') to recognise and accept the sovereign's arbitrations in order to escape social anarchy. To reject the absolute power of the sovereign is, in effect, to opt for social anarchy, a 'state of warre', as Hobbes calls it.[19] Hobbes' seductive doctrine of sovereignty has provided a very

[18] An old but still valuable study is that by James Barr, *Fundamentalism*, London, SCM Press, 1977. However, Barr limits his enquiry to fundamentalism in Christianity and, within Christianity, to Protestantism. For a Roman Catholic approach see Thomas F. O'Meara, *Fundamentalism: A Catholic Perspective*, New Jersey, Paulist Press, 1990. For a sociological view of the social and political implications of American and Iranian fundamentalism see Martin Riesebrodt, *Pious Passion: The Emergence of Modern Fundamentalism in the U. S. and Iran*, Berkeley, University of California Press, 1993. See also Martin E. Marty, *Fundamentalists Observed*, Chicago, 1991. This is the first part of a five volume study by the Fundamentalist Project of the US Academy of Arts and Sciences.

[19] Thomas Hobbes, *Leviathan*, London, J. M. Dent, 1949.

powerful model that has been used in other fields, but its influence has been largely disastrous.

Many of Hobbes' critics have pointed out how paradoxical his doctrine of sovereignty is, in that it demands that, in order to escape social anarchy, we must put ourselves in the hands of a sovereign with absolute and unconditional power against whom we have no appeal or redress. In effect, we consent to give up our power of consent. The same paradox affects any attempt to make the interpretation by church authorities final and absolute. We recognise that the scriptures (the Word of God) need human interpretation and mediation, but we are then asked to accept that the authoritative interpretations of the church authorities escape the need for interpretation, as though they were not subject to the ordinary processes of logic, and the rules of meaning were miraculously waivable.

Acknowledging that there cannot be an absolutely final (or 'Hobbesian') arbiter of authoritative meaning in a religious tradition, does not mean that valid interpretations cannot be made and that we land in some kind of interpretational anarchy akin to Hobbes' 'state of warre'. None of our courts of law – even our supreme courts – have unconditional Hobbesian power, save in the pragmatic sense that for practical purposes (the talking has to stop and a decision has to be handed down) we *deem* their decisions to be final. And yet, of course, for the most part valid interpretations are made and the legal system continues. The same is true in any religious tradition. We are not confronted with a stark choice between either accepting an absolute authority (and denying human mediation), or ending in interpretive anarchy or the wilder forms of sectarianism.

Scriptural fundamentalism and institutional fundamentalism are two forms or modalities of a deeper and more basic religious pathology which I have characterised as the attempt to deny the role of human invention in religion. Characterisations of contemporary varieties of fundamentalism usually fix upon the fundamentalists' conservative fear of change, their desire for 'absolutes' in belief and practice, and their wish to safeguard 'the truth' from relativising forces of all kinds. Typically, it has been said, this leads to a stance of 'oppositionalism' where the champions of the true faith do continual battle with the enemy, usually seen as 'liberals' or relativists or as the agents of malign forces both secular and supernatural.[20]

These characterisations are, no doubt, true of many forms of fundamentalism at the present time, but, in my view, they are secondary and do not reveal the root of fundamentalism which, as has been said, is the attempt to deny the place of human invention in religion. Ultimately, fundamentalism is animated by a profound distrust or even fear of the human, and by an impossible desire that the divine should be kept pure and untainted by anything human.

As we have seen, there is a similar distrust at work in the attempt to create a Christian ethics which would supplant the ethics of human enquiry. Even the official Roman Catholic position, which relies on a version of the 'natural law' theory of ethics, nevertheless makes ethics subject to the teaching authority of the church, and, in effect, transforms the basic ethical precepts into 'truths of faith'. In other words, we cannot really trust ordinary human enquiry and reflection in the ethical realm.

As against this, we have to recognise the autonomy of the ethical order, and accept the fact that we – Christians and non-Christians alike – have to make do with the ordinary ethics of human enquiry. As was noted before, this is, in fact, what most Christians do in their reflections on ethical issues. When one looks at what are put forward as examples of 'Christian ethics', it can be seen that they are for the most part exercises (some unexceptional, some dubious) in ordinary ethics.

This recognition of the autonomy of the ethical order means that so-called moral theology will no longer be concerned, at least directly, with issues that arise in the ethics of human enquiry, any more than theology is directly concerned with issues that arise in the autonomous areas of philosophy or science. Instead, moral theology will focus its attention on the Christian way of perfection, and will have much more to say about the likes of Eckhart and the so-called mystics than about the ethics of human reproduction. The Sermon on the Mount will no longer be seen as a set of

---

[20] See Martin E. Marty, 'What is Fundamentalism?: Theological Perspectives', in Hans Küng and J. Moltmann eds. *Fundamentalism as an Ecumenical Challenge*, *Concilium*, 1992/3, 3–13.

'counsels of perfection' meant only for a spiritual elite, but as a guide for all Christians.[21]

FINALE

My discussion in this book has been concerned with the indispensable role of human creativity and imagination in religion. Instead of seeing the human interpretation of 'revelation' as in some way obscuring or distorting the original purity and immediacy of a given revelation, I have tried to show that the latter is always and necessarily mediated by human reception and understanding. Religion is always very much what we make of it. The hope that we can discover a primordial 'deposit of faith' underlying the accretions of interpretation and 'tradition' is an illusion, and, so I have argued, a dangerous illusion. Ultimately, it is an attempt to escape our responsibility for creatively and freely responding to the acts of grace we call 'revelation'.

Once we have accepted the inescapably inventive character of religion, we can then make some kind of sense of a brute and undeniable fact which has always been seen as an irrational 'scandal' in the past, namely the multiplicity and diversity of religions or expressions of the divine. Instead of seeing the radical diversity and variety of religions as due – using Newman's words in another context – to 'some terrible aboriginal calamity' or to a theological Tower of Babel, I have tried to show that that diversity should rather be seen as a manifestation of the extraordinary fecundity and richness and unpredictability of the order of grace and of the creative human responses to the various revelations of the divine.

In a sense, this is to put in question the great Neoplatonic metaphor that has dominated western religious thinking for so long – the divine One expressed or refracted in its many manifestations. Instead, it is the effervescent 'many-ness' of the divine which is, so to speak, the primary religious datum from which we must begin.

Of course, this way of seeing things raises formidable philosophical and theological problems, but I have not been able to consider

---

[21] See Mark O'Keefe, 'Catholic Moral Theology and Christian Spirituality', *New Theological Review*, 7, 1994, 60–73.

those problems here. I have simply tried to show the consequences of taking two obvious facts seriously: on the one hand, the role of human invention in religion, and, on the other hand, the irreducible diversity of religions or expressions of the acts of grace we call revelation.

Aristotle tells the charming story of some people visiting Herakleitos at his home. They found the sage sitting in the kitchen by the stove and they hesitated to enter. But Herakleitos said to them: 'Come in. Don't be afraid. There are gods even here.'[22]

Herakleitos the Obscure is a dangerous patron to invoke, and all kinds of outlandish readings have been foisted upon his fragmentary writings, but I would like to think of my approach here as a generally 'Herakleitean' one.

[22] *Parts of Animals*, 645a: 19–23.

Index

Albertus Magnus, Saint, 123, 141–2
amawurena, 75
Ancestor Spirits, 15–16, 47, 56, 65, 67, 72, 74, 75
anonymous Christians, 42
anthropology of anthropology, 51–3
Apologists, Christian, 25
Aquinas, Saint Thomas, 129–33, 134, 141
Aranda people, 72, 76
Aristotle, 81, 84, 89, 124–5, 129–30, 143, 153
art,
    as a family resemblance concept, 2, 20
    Australian Aboriginal, 70
    Oceanic, 21
Aubert, Roger, 108
Augustine, Saint, 112, 121, 123
Australian Aboriginal
    languages, 55
    religions, 14–16, 47, **51–79**
    secrecy, 69–70
    social groupings, 56–7, 62
    'women's business', 66–7

Babel, 30, 152
Barth, Karl, 116
Beguines, 142
Bell, Diane, 67
Bernanos, George, 10
Blake, William, 84, 144
Bossuet, J. B., 120
Brown, Peter, 20
Buddhism, 33, 34, 36, 42–3, 47, 77, 102
Burkert, Walter, 7.

Cahill, Lisa Sowle, 112, 114
Catechism of the Catholic Church, 115

Carter, Paul, 76
Chesterton, G. K., 22
Christian ethics, **105–37**
    changes in, 119–27
    concept of, 17–18
    criticism of, 151
Christianity,
    universal and local aspects, 82–3
    and tradition, 92–5
    and world religions, 41–3
Clifford, James, 51–3, 68
conscience, 121
Corbin, Henry, 44–5

Dalai Lama, 34, 42–3, 46
Davidson, Iain, 15
Davies, Oliver, 37, 143
Declaration on Religious Freedom, 121–2
de las Casas, Bartolome, 25
De Libera, Alain, 37, 143
democratic capitalism, 116
demonic, the, 8. 21
Dennett, Daniel C., 6
deposit of faith, 152
Derrida, Jacques, 21, 28, 30, 86, 88
development of revelation, **95–101**
diversity of revelations, 13–14, **23–49**
    endemic feature of religions, 14, 152
    scandal of, 23–7
divine, the, 1, 140, 148, 151
Dogmatic Constitution on Divine Revelation, 98
Dominicans, 142–3
double effect, principle, 132
Duchesne, Louis, 95
Dulles, Avery, 23
Dunstan, Gordon, 124
Durkheim, Emile, 59 , 72–6

Dreaming
  In Australian Aboriginal religions, 64,
    72–6

Eckhart, Meister, 20, 35–6, 141–4
Eco, Umberto, 13
ecumenical movement, 27–30
Eliade, Mircea, 66
Elkin, A. P., 66, 73
Emptiness, Buddhist, 47
experience, mystical, 35–6, 141–3

family resemblance concepts, 2
Feuerbach, Luwig, 5
Fish, Stanley, 87
Foucault, Michel, 86
foundationalism, 85–8
Frazer, Sir James, 58
Freud, Sigmund, 5
Fuchs, Josef, 108, 119
fundamentalism, 7, 65, 100–1, 116, 140,
    149–51

Galey, Jean Claude, 102
Geertz, Clifford, 87
Geluk tradition in Buddhism, 42–3
'good pagans', 25
Greek ethics, 112–14
Gregory XVI, Pope, 121, 123
Gustafson, James T., 106, 116

Hadot, Pierre, 3, 113
Hale, Ken, 65
Hegel G. W. F., 81, 87
Herakleitos, 153
Hick, John, 41,43
Hinduism, 77, 102–3
Hobbes, Thomas, 149–50
human embryo, 122–5
human nature, 128–9
Humanae Vitae, 133
hylomorphism, 124–5

Ibn Sina, 37, 125, 143
idealistic perfectionism, 108–12, 117
*Instruction on Respect for Human Life in its
    Origins,* 122
interpretive–inventive perspective,
    12–13
intrinsically evil acts, 132
invention, concept of, 5, 9, 10–2, 140
Islam, 25, 39–40, 77

James, William, 20, 140
Jawoyn people, 75
Judaism, 25, 31, 39, 77, 94, 109–10

Kant, Immanuel, 29, 53
Katrei, Sister, 142
Keen, Ian, 71
Kierkegaard, Søren, 81
Kingdom of God, 1, 14, 146
Knitter, Paul, 48
Kuhn, Thomas, 34, 88
Küng, Hans, 1, 14

language, 13, 91–2
law,
    Australian Aboriginal, 72–3
    Jewish, 109–10
Leiris, Michel, 53
Lévi-Strauss, Claude, 14, 51, 61, 86
Lévy-Bruhl, Lucien, 61
Lewis, Bernard, 39–40
Loisy, Alfred, 95

MacIntyre, Alastair, 35–6
magisterium, 99–100, 134
Mahoney, John, 107
Mardudjara people, 63, 65
Marx, Karl, 5, 6
Mauss, Marcel, 60
Meeks, Wayne A., 111
Moehler, Johann Adam, 94
modernism, 100
moral theology, 18–9, 107–8
Morphy, Howard, 62, 66, 69
Muggletonians, 144–6
Mulvaney, D. J., 54, 59, 63
Murray, John Courtney, 96, 122

natural law, 18, 107, 115, 127–32
    Aquinas on, 129–31
    Catholic church as interpreter of,
        132–6
Nelson, Daniel Mark, 130
Neoplatonism, 34, 45–7, 113, 152
Newman, John Henry, 96, 152
Nietzsche, Friedrich, 5
Noonan, John T., 119–22
numinous, the, 68, 140
Nussbaum, Martha, 17, 90

Old Testament, 25, 31
Otto, Rudolf, 68

Pannikar, Raimundo, 44, 47
pathological developments in religions, 4,
    21–2, 147–8
Paul VI, Pope, 133
Paul, Saint, 82, 111–12, 120, 128, 146
Philo, 111
philosophical ways of life, 3, 113
philosophy of religion, 1, 4
phronesis, 111
pilgrimage, 102
Pitjantjatjara people, 67
Pius IX, Pope, 97, 121, 123
Plato, 128
pluralism, 32, 44, 99, 136
practical wisdom, 130
Pre-Raphaelite movement, 146
primal religions, 31, 139
Proclus, 45
prudence, 130–1
Pseudo-Dionysius, 37
Putnam, Hilary, 86

Qur'ān, 10, 33

Radcliffe-Brown, A. R., 62–3, 66
Rahner, Karl, 26, 41, 42, 97, 99
reception hermeneutics, 11
relativism, 88–91
religion,
    coercion in, 8
    concept of, 1
    definition of, 2
    freedom in, 8
    intolerance in, 8
    persistence of, 21
revelation,
    concept of, 9
    diversity of, 13–4, 23–7, 32
    gratuitous character of, 10
    response to, 10
Rivers, W. H. R., 62
Roman Catholic Church,
    and freedom of conscience, 100
    and institutional fundamentalism, 100
    and moral theology, 107–8
    and natural law, **127–35**
    and the human embryo, 122–5
Rosaldo, R., 63
Rose, Deborah Bird, 74, 77

sacred sites, 102
Sartre, Jean Paul, 5, 148

Schillebeeckx, Edward, 16–17
Schuon, Fritjof, 24
scientism, 6–7
Second Vatican Council, 83, 98, 100,
    121
secrecy, 69–70
Secretariat for Non-Christian Religions,
    26
sects, 144–6
Seneca, 113, 128
sensus fidelium, 90
Sermon on the Mount, 108–11, 136, 152
slavery, 120–1
Spence, Jonathan, 144
Spencer, Baldwin, 58–9, 63, 72
spiritual exercises, 3
Stace, W. T., 35–8
Stanner, W. E. H., 62, 66, 79
Stoics, 128
Swain, Tony, 66, 75, 77, 102
Sykes, Stephen, 94

Taiping movement, 142
Taoism, 102
theory independence, 37–8
Thomas, Nicholas, 21
Thompson, E. P., 84–5, 144–6
Tonkinson, Robert, 63
Torah, 10
totemism, 61–2, 64
tradition in religions, 16–17, 92–5
Trinitarian theology, 49
Turner, David, 66, 74

'Universal reason', 128
usury, 120

Via negativa, 78–9
vice lists, 111
virginity, 146–7

Wallace, Noel, 67
Warlpiri people, 65, 75, 77
Weber, Max, 29, 109
Williams, Bernard, 87
Wittgenstein, Ludwig, 2, 86
women, equality of, 126

Yarralin people, 74
Yolngu people, 56, 66, 69, 71

Zaehner, R. C., 39